PITTSBURGH SPORTS
IN THE 1970s

PITTSBURGH SPORTS
IN THE 1970s

TRAGEDIES, TRIUMPHS AND CHAMPIONSHIPS

DAVID FINOLI, TOM ROONEY, TIM ROONEY,
CHRIS FLETCHER AND FRANK GARLAND

THE
History
PRESS

Published by The History Press
Charleston, SC
www.historypress.com

First published 2023

Manufactured in the United States

ISBN 9781467155007

Library of Congress Control Number: 2023937176

Notice: The information in this book is true and complete to the best of our
knowledge. It is offered without guarantee on the part of the author or The
History Press. The author and The History Press disclaim all liability in
connection with the use of this book.

To Franco Harris.
Your legacy means so much more to this city than just a catch
on December 23, 1972. May you rest in peace.

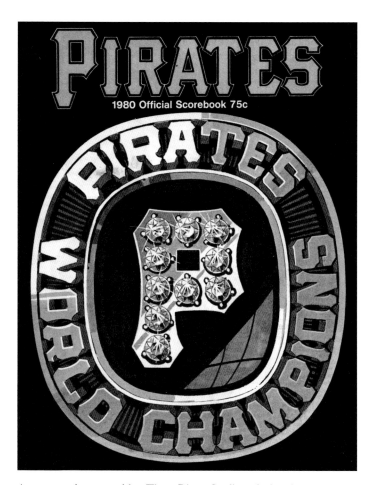

A program that was sold at Three Rivers Stadium during the 1980 season commemorating the team's memorable 1979 world championship run. *Photo courtesy of David Finoli.*

CONTENTS

ACKNOWLEDGEMENTS

Creating a book is certainly an effort that brings the passion of the subject out in the people who tell the story. This one was no different for the five authors who tell the story of the greatest decade a city has ever experienced when it comes to its sports teams. As much effort as it took from us to put this book together, it could not have been completed without the help of others.

With the time we put in over and above our normal workdays, a thank-you goes out to our families and friends for the support they gave us throughout the process. This couldn't have been achieved without them.

There was Duquesne University's David Saba, E.J. Borghetti of the University of Pittsburgh and Jim Trdinich of the Pittsburgh Pirates, who generously allowed us to use the photos in the book. Their photo donations are very much appreciated.

We also would like to thank Rob Ruck and Dave Hansen, along with many others who helped us with the various chapters of this book.

Finally, we'd like to thank The History Press, especially our acquisition editor, Banks Smither, who has been an incredible partner for all of the books the group and I have written for this outstanding publisher, of which this is the fifteenth I've personally had the pleasure of doing with them. Without the help of all, this book would not have been a possibility.

DF

INTRODUCTION

The 1970s in the Steel City was not always a time its citizens remember fondly. The steel mills that employed so many were beginning to close at a rapid pace as the inflation and gas shortages that gripped the entire nation were being felt in Western Pennsylvania, too. It was important that people had diversions to take their minds off their troubles, and luckily, we had our sports teams, many of which were going through golden eras, creating the feeling that at any given time, a championship could be won.

Championship parades were almost a yearly event on the local calendars, and by the end of the decade, the nation was calling us something we already knew we were: City of Champions. It was truly amazing what we had the chance to experience.

For the better part of the first 40 years of their existence, the Pittsburgh Steelers were lovable losers—though calling them lovable may have been a stretch. If there was a last place to be had, the Steelers would find a way to take that spot more times than not. They had been in exactly one playoff game, at Forbes Field in 1947, after they tied their cross-state rivals the Philadelphia Eagles for the Eastern Division title. Amid a controversy over if and how they'd get paid for the game, let's say our hometown boys weren't exactly focused on getting to the NFL Championship contest. They fell meekly to the Eagles 21–0. It would be 25 years until they had the chance to do it all again. After winning their first championship of any kind, the 1972 Central Division crown, they had the opportunity to play in another postseason game. Down late to the Oakland Raiders 7–6, it

The 1976 Pitt Panther football team completed their miraculous four-year run when the 1–10 1972 squad became the undefeated national champions four years later. This is the program that was sold at the Sugar Bowl the day Pitt defeated Georgia 27–3 to capture their ninth national crown. *Photo courtesy of David Finoli.*

looked like another case of SOS (Same Old Steelers) when Franco Harris rescued them and exorcised the franchise's demons with a little play called the Immaculate Reception that won the contest 13–7. The Steelers would go on to unprecedented success, winning four Super Bowl titles in six years by the time the decade ended.

While current fans have come to expect many disappointments with our local baseball club, the Pittsburgh Pirates, in the 1970s they were among the most talented franchises in the game. As an organization, they were one of the first to aggressively go after Latin American talent and had a farm system that few if any rivaled. Led by perhaps the greatest Latin American player in the history of the game, Roberto Clemente, they won the East Division in 1970, then took it one step further the following season with the franchise's fourth world championship against the powerful Baltimore Orioles. By the time we were looking 1980 in the face, they had captured six division titles in the decade and another World Series title as the 1970s closed out—ironically, once again in Memorial Stadium against the hated Orioles. If that was enough, it would be truly a decade to remember, but there was more.

As the decade began, football at the University of Pittsburgh had become a joke. After finishing 1–10 in 1972, they were considered arguably the worst major football program in the land. That's when the powers that be at the school—namely chancellor Wesley Posvar and the school's athletic director, Cas Myslinski—loosened the entrance requirements and recruiting rules for athletes and hired an exciting young coach from Iowa State by the name of Johnny Majors. Miraculously, within four years, they finished undefeated and won the program's ninth national championship before Majors went back home to Tennessee. Instead of crumbling, they hired his former defensive coordinator, Jackie Sherrill, to man the ship, and Sherrill took them to new heights. Beginning in 1979, they went 11–1 for three consecutive seasons and were now among the nation's elite teams on an annual basis.

There was so much more. Carnegie-Mellon University had one of the country's top Division III football programs, while Westminster was a legendary one at the NAIA Division II level, winning back-to-back national titles in 1976 and 1977. The Triangles of World Team Tennis captured a memorable crown in 1975, the same year that a local minor league hockey team by the name of the Johnstown Jets also won a championship—and inspired a movie by the name of *Slap Shot*. There was also success with the indoor soccer team the Pittsburgh Spirit, a local national club football championship by Duquesne University and several good seasons by the school's basketball program to go along with a memorable campaign with Pitt hoops in 1974.

It wasn't all joy, though, that people experienced. The Penguins, just when it was thought they were joining the championship group, lost a heartbreaking series against the Islanders in 1975 and never recovered—hell, they almost went belly-up. The Pirate dynasty was derailed on a couple occasions, first by a famed wild pitch in 1972 that took a sure victory from them in the NLCS against the Reds, then a pitcher for the Phils by the name of Randy Lerch almost singlehandedly took their division title aspirations from them and became a verb (more on that in chapter 37). Worse yet were the tragic deaths of loved athletes that seemed to happen too often, starting in 1971, when the savior of the franchise for the Pittsburgh Penguins, Michel Brière, was killed in an automobile accident. Then we all knew where we were when we heard the news that Roberto Clemente's plane went down on New Year's Eve 1972 in the Atlantic Ocean while trying to deliver much-needed supplies to earthquake-ravaged Nicaragua. Local hero Bob Moose was killed in an accident in 1976, the same year beloved manager Danny Murtaugh sadly died after a stroke at 59 years old.

We shared the joys together and comforted each other in times of tragedy. It's a bond we formed that we still see so much of today: the love we have for our teams. All these special moments are captured in this book. Enjoy the memories reading them that we certainly did writing about them.

DF

CHAPTER 1

1970: A PALACE FOR THE FANS

THREE RIVERS STADIUM OPENS ITS DOORS

By David Finoli

I t was early afternoon on July 16, 1970, when my father came into the den to talk about the baseball game he was going to that evening. The Cincinnati Reds were coming to Pittsburgh to face the Pirates, and he was so thrilled to be going. He went into song and verse about how Forbes Field was an uncomfortable place to watch a game. How it smelled like urine and stale beer. How Three Rivers would be a joy to watch a game at, with all its modern amenities. It would be a festive event, a sparkling new palace for the fans to enjoy Pirates and Steeler games as the 1970s were about to commence. It was a great way to open up the new decade, but Three Rivers Stadium should have have opened its doors quite a few years earlier.

The year was 1948, and the Bucs were coming off a surprising second-place finish in a season that would be the only joy the club enjoyed over the next decade. It was that year that the new owners of the team, led by the Galbreath family, decided that Forbes Field was antiquated. Seven years later, the city fathers agreed, and the Allegheny Conference on Community Development put together a committee to study the situation and develop a plan in 1955. In 1958, it looked like a new facility was only a few years away when the University of Pittsburgh decided to buy Forbes Field, with the intent of building new school facilities when a new stadium was completed and Forbes Field could be dismantled.

Pitt gave the Pirates $2 million for the land and agreed to allow Forbes to remain until 1963, when all agreed a stadium would be completed.

After over a decade of disagreements, budget overflows and several other obstacles that prevented the building of a new multipurpose stadium in Pittsburgh, Three Rivers Stadium finally opened on July 16, 1970. *Photo courtesy of the Pittsburgh Pirates.*

Unfortunately, by 1963, a new facility was no closer to being built than it had been when the idea was formulated eight years earlier. It was to be a stadium that would house both the Pirates and the Steelers. The teams, the city and the county all argued about who would pay for it. They chose a site on the north side of the city, a 48-acre plot of land where abandoned warehouses and discarded railroad tracks lay—and oh yeah, had no infrastructure to house the 50,000 proposed fans that would hopefully attend these games. Add to the mix two Allegheny County commissioners, William McClelland and John McGrady, who were vehemently opposed to spending county money on the plan, and one could now understand why such an endeavor was taking so long.

Only half of the $45 million plan was meant for the stadium; the rest was to construct hotels, shops and restaurants, none of which would be built until Acrisure Stadium (Heinz Field) and PNC Park replaced Three Rivers Stadium to begin the 21st century. Frustration was felt by all parties, with the two teams threatening to move if the deal could not be completed and the university wanting to finally move forward with its plans to expand at the site where Forbes Field stood.

Finally, in 1967, the situation finally started moving forward: the badly needed new infrastructure was being built, and plans for the stadium were being formulated. There was one plan to have the new facility built on top of a bridge and another approach that would have had the open back of the stadium looking over the city—just like PNC Park. When everything appeared to be moving ahead, the budget reared its ugly head.

It was a budget that was made years before and apparently never amended to take inflation into account. The lowest bid by the contractors was $12 million over the proposed budget, causing more issues, of course. Eventually, the construction firm of Huber-Hunt and Nichols was able to reduce the cost by $10 million, partly due to the agreement that they would use the so-called cookie-cutter design being used to build new stadiums in Cincinnati, Philadelphia and Atlanta, a basic round design that made it difficult to tell them apart.

Even though construction began in 1968, there were still many issues left to conquer. The bridge built to take the 50,000 fans to the new stadium, eventually named the Fort Duquesne Bridge, was left only three-quarters of the way built, eventually being named the Bridge to Nowhere, until the city came up with $3 million to complete it. Labor strikes also delayed its completion, which was hoped for by opening day in 1970; it would not be done until mid-season. Finally, on July 16, 1970, it was ready to go, complete with an artificial turf called Tartan Turf that would make baseball a much faster game, as the ball would move much more quickly than on a normal grass field.

The Pirates may have lost that day against the Reds, but Dad was duly impressed—at least temporarily (45 years later, he would tell me how great Forbes Field was and how ghastly Three Rivers turned out). Both the Pirates and the Steelers—and, at times, the University of Pittsburgh—now had a brand-new stadium to lead them into the 1970s. While it may not have been an architectural delight, it brought both teams incredible success in the decade and truly became, at least for 10 years, a true field of dreams for sports fans in Pittsburgh.

CHAPTER 2

1970: THAT SEVENTIES SHOW

THE PIRATES STARTED A DECADE OF EXCELLENCE IN THE 1970s WITH A SEASON THAT HINTED OF THINGS TO COME

By Chris Fletcher

The Pittsburgh Pirates opened the 1960s with a bang, capturing the first World Series crown of the decade in rather spectacular style, thanks to Bill Mazeroski's famed ninth-inning home run in game seven. For many, it was the sign that a drought dating to 1925 would soon finally be over and the team would have another decade of excellence when players like Pie Traynor, the Waner brothers and Max Carey would lead a Corsair squad that showed consistent excellence. But unfortunately, the franchise would not hit such heights again in the remainder of the '60s.

The Bucs were competitive, averaging 85 wins per year, which isn't bad. Unfortunately, despite having three Hall of Famers for the better part of the decade in Roberto Clemente, Willie Stargell and Bill Mazeroski, they only managed one title. One reason: the competition was fierce. The Pirates had to compete against two dynamic, dominant teams: the St. Louis Cardinals and the Los Angeles Dodgers. Both teams had star-studded pitching staffs that trumped the Pirates' big bats over a long season.

The closest the Bucs came to a pennant was 1966. They were in the race until the last week before slipping into third place, four games behind the pennant-winning Dodgers. The Pirates even printed World Series tickets, which are hot collectors' items if you're lucky enough to come across them.

So, when the league expanded and reorganized in 1969, creating two divisions—a National League East and a National League West—and adding one more postseason spot, it immediately brought hope that the

The 1970 Pittsburgh Pirates. Starting the year playing in Forbes Field, the Bucs would move to their new facility, Three Rivers Stadium, on July 16. They would eventually capture their first Eastern Division crown that season. *Photo courtesy of the Pittsburgh Pirates.*

latest drought was about to end. It didn't happen that year, as the Miracle Mets won the inaugural NL East, but there was considerable hope on the horizon entering the 1970s.

The new decade brought an influx of young talent that was beginning to gel. General manager Joe Brown put together a strong farm system that was sending solid players to the majors. Bob Robertson showed tremendous raw power at first. Dave Cash was ready to supplant Maz at second. Richie Hebner became a fan favorite at third with a strong bat that made up for an erratic glove. Young outfielders Al Oliver and Gene Clines pushed for more playing time. Manny Sanguillen provided stability, great defense and a solid bat behind the plate. Pitching, a Bucs bugaboo during most of the '60s, improved with the addition of Luke Walker and an emerging Dock Ellis.

But an even more exciting sign of new hopes of success was the opening of a shiny new ballpark: Three Rivers Stadium. But that would have to wait until mid-season because of a series of construction delays.

Pittsburgh started well, taking three of four from the defending champion Mets and racing out to a 9–4 record. But then came a 3–10 stretch, including being swept in Cincinnati, giving up 24 runs in three games to the Big Red Machine.

The Pirates reached Memorial Day with a record of just 20–23. Fortunately, the rest of the NL was struggling, too. Despite playing poorly, the Bucs were only three and a half games back of the Chicago Cubs, with the Mets and Cardinals nestled in between.

The team received a boost after the All-Star break with the opening of Three Rivers Stadium. With the stadium's artificial turf, state-of-the-art scoreboard and less cavernous dimensions than Forbes Field, the Pirates, long known for their hitting, would be even more dangerous. In the new park, Stargell became even more of a threat. Clemente would also benefit from balls scooting on the Tartan Turf—a bug on the rug, as Pirates announcer Bob Prince called them.

Still, the Pirates were streaky. A 7–1 start to August was followed by another 3–10 stretch, but they captured the division with an 89–73 record and a five-game lead over the Cubs.

The Pirates were a good team, with some glaring deficiencies. The pitching staff didn't have any true aces, yet it was third in the league in ERA. Its strength was a deep bullpen—with Walker who both started and relieved (winning 15 games), Dave Giusti (9 wins and 26 saves) and Bruce Dal Canton (9 wins in relief). Offensively, it was a mixed bag. While they led the league in slugging, the Pirates were middle of the league in home runs and not exactly patient at the plate and were last in drawing walks. What this meant was that for the Pirates to win, they had to get the big hit in the clutch.

Their opponents in the League Championship Series, the Reds, had bulldozed the rest of the league, winning the division by 15 games en route to rolling up 102 wins. Had this been 1968, the Pirates would have once again missed the postseason. Heading into the best-of-five series, the Pirates had been 4–8 against the Reds.

The series opened in Pittsburgh, and game one was a classic playoff game. Bucs starter Ellis worked out of trouble several times, holding Cincy scoreless through nine. Unfortunately, the Pirates couldn't score off Reds starter Gary Nolan, either. In the bottom of the eighth, Stargell led off with a double, but Nolan ended the inning with two strikeouts. In the ninth, Freddie Patek was thrown out trying to steal.

The Reds broke the tie in the 10th, thanks to a lead-off pinch-hit triple by Cincy's Ty Cline. Pete Rose singled him in, and the Reds added two insurance runs for a 3–0 win.

Game two was more of the same. Walker started and battled through some tight spots while the Pirates still were unable to get the big hit. Cincinnati's speed was the difference, with center fielder Bobby Tolan taking over. Tolan singled to left, stole second and then took third on a throwing error before scoring on a wild pitch. In his next at bat, Tolan launched a solo blast to put the Reds up 2–0. He added another run, scoring on Tony Perez's double as the Reds cruised to a 3–1 win.

As the series shifted to Cincinnati, the Pirates faced elimination. They took their first lead of the series, scoring in the first inning to open a 1–0 lead. But again, the team failed to get the big hit, squandering opportunities. Back-to-back homers by Reds sluggers Tony Perez and Johnny Bench gave them a lead they wouldn't relinquish and a series sweep.

Despite being outmatched, the Pirates were in each game, but it was the Reds who consistently got the clutch hit or the key out on their way to the pennant. Still, the series foreshadowed a successful stretch for the Pirates in the 1970s. The team would go on to win the division six times and raise two World Series banners. And it also marked the beginning of a postseason rivalry with the Reds, whom they would face three more times. These two teams would battle for NL superiority in one of the most successful decades in Pirates history.

CHAPTER 3

1970: YOI, DOUBLE YOI AND MAYBE EVEN TRIPLE YOI

MYRON COPE BECOMES A STEELER LEGEND

By David Finoli

Often, when listening to Pittsburgh icon Myron Cope, you'd hear him bellow the word *yoi* when emphasizing a thought. If he was pretty excited about something, he'd back it up with a double yoi. On the rare occasion when he was stunned beyond explanation, he'd dole out a triple yoi, and your day would be made. While Cope was most known for throwing out yois here and there, there were so many other memorable things he did and statements he made that they could fill this entire book. Without a doubt, he is part of the Holy Trinity of Pittsburgh sports announcers, along with the Penguins' Mike Lange and the Bucs' Bob Prince. His career as the legendary color man for the Steelers began with an announcement in the *Pittsburgh Post-Gazette* by TV writer Edward L. Blank on July 24, 1970, exclaiming the news that Cope would join play-by-play man Jack Fleming in the booth, a partnership that would last 24 years.

Before Cope became an NFL color man and local Pittsburgh talk show king, he was a writer, one of the best in the business, first for the *Post-Gazette*, then for *Sports Illustrated*, along with being the author of two superb books and eventually a third, much later on in his career.

A little-known fact about Myron was that Cope wasn't his original name. It was Myron Kopelman. When he started at the Pittsburgh paper, a city editor by the name of Joe Shuman decided there were too many Jewish

When you become an icon in the city of Pittsburgh, you get a bobblehead made of yourself. Myron Cope is an icon; this is his bobblehead. Cope was more than just the memorable color man on Steeler radio broadcasts; he also had a widely popular talk show that any self-respecting Pittsburgh sports fan never missed. *Photo courtesy of David Finoli.*

reporters there, and as Cope stated in his book *Double Yoi*, Shuman went on to say, "And on top of that we've got several Germans whose names might be taken for Jewish." Intent on coming up with a more generic byline for his new reporter, he flipped through the phone book and came to the *C*s, where he saw the last name Cope, and the legendary name was born.

Eventually, Myron found his way to *Sports Illustrated*, where he became an award-winning writer. In 1963, his article on the then Cassius Clay (Muhammad Ali) won him the EP Dutton Award for best magazine writing in the country. An article he wrote on Howard Cosell captured him on the list of the top 50 articles ever written in *Sports Illustrated* for its 50th anniversary. He also was known for his article on Roberto Clemente in the 1960s pointing out that the Pirate superstar may have been a hypochondriac.

Despite a nasally, high-pitched voice that didn't seem like it was meant for the airwaves, Cope began to do sports commentary from his home for WTAE-AM in Pittsburgh in 1968 before beginning his famed talk show on the same station five years later. It wasn't only the unique voice that drew people to listen but also his unique opinions on local sports matters; his Christmas sports carols he would premiere on local TV sportscasts; the lab coat he'd don, looking into a microscope as "Dr." Cope broke down a team's strengths and weaknesses; and the way he said things that drew radio listeners to him by the masses. He was number one in his time slot from the day he began the show until he retired.

As popular as Cope's radio show was and as iconic as he was in the Steelers booth, it was an invention he came up with in 1975 that he was arguably most famous for: the Terrible Towel. Before the team's first playoff game at Three Rivers Stadium that year against the Baltimore Colts, a radio executive at WTAE challenged Myron to come up with a gimmick for the game. Apprehensive at first, Cope began to think of ideas, along with some of the management at the station. A black costume mask with Chuck Noll's favorite saying, "Whatever it takes," on it was thought about first as a giveaway.

Finally, WTAE's vice president for sales, Larry Garrett, quipped about a towel. According to Cope in his autobiography, he said, "Yes, we could call it the Terrible Towel. And I could go on the radio and television proclaiming 'The Terrible Towel is poised to strike.'" It was the beginning of an iconic item. Steelers fans across the globe own multiple towels in their team arsenal, and its magic powers have led the team to five Super Bowl championships (yes, they won the first without it). It has done wonderful things for the community, too. In 1996, the legendary Steeler announcer turned over the rights to the towel to the Allegheny Valley School, which helps children with intellectual disabilities, including his son Danny, who has severe autism. To date, the towel has helped the school raise millions of dollars.

Cope has done so much for the community. He came up with the term "the Immaculate Reception" on his radio show for Franco's memorable play. He was the first broadcaster chosen by the Pro Football Hall of Fame to be on their selection committee. But mainly he was a source of entertainment for us.

He retired in 2005 after 35 years in the booth. Three years later, we were crushed on learning of his passing on February 27, 2008. He was missed by fans, media and players alike. Former Steeler Gerry Mullins said in an article on Steelertakeaways.com, "You were one of the guys we trusted. We could talk to guys like you and Myron Cope and we knew you weren't going to throw us under the bus. I'd tell Myron something and he'd say 'a little bird told me' when he'd use the item on his show. You guys weren't out to hurt us. That wasn't true with some of the media."

His partner after Jack Fleming, Bill Hillgrove, recalled in the same article, "Myron Cope would not have fun now. They aren't allowed to be characters. I liked it when the wackos could be wackos. But I do understand. There's too much money now and it's had a profound effect on how they can act.

"Steelers fans see the outfits and the videos of him waving the towels, but he was dead serious as a writer. He must have had special glasses, because he had the uncanny ability to see the humor in things. I always said he could see the humor in the Lord's Prayer.

"I remember when I roomed with him, he would work forever in the first word of his sentences, getting up and walking around the room, looking for the right word. He would tell me that the difference between the right word and the ok one was the difference between lightning and lightning bug. That always stuck with me."

However you choose to remember Myron, most likely it is in the fondest of ways for a career in the Steelers booth that began in the fall of 1970.

CHAPTER 4

1970–71: THE PENGUINS' TERRIFIC SPRING TURNS FROM TRIUMPH TO TRAGEDY

By Tom Rooney

The National Hockey League doubled its roster of teams when six new franchises were added for the 1967–68 season. Pittsburgh was one of the new teams. And in more than the first two decades of their existence, those Pittsburgh Penguins mostly couldn't fly! They made it to the NHL Stanley Cup Semifinals just once, the third season, 1969–70. And actually, the prospect of even more imminent success seemed very good in 1970. That optimism helped blunt the disappointment of having just lost a tough six-game battle with the hated St. Louis Blues. The Penguins had been but one step away, crowds thronged to the playoff games with the Blues and the team was seemingly skating in the right direction.

But that 1970 flourish was a false spring. The optimism centered on newly arrived young players and was epitomized by a 20-year-old shooting star who seemed to come out of nowhere. But just as fast as a breakaway, he was gone. Michel Brière, the precocious little third-round draft choice, first-year pro center from an obscure outpost in the province of Quebec, would never see another season after a tragic car accident soon after returning from Pittsburgh from the playoffs. Triumph tripped by tragedy in short order, and the best was not yet to come, really, until a player whose name translated to "the best" (Lemieux) arrived in the 1980s.

First, a little scene-setting from a man who attended and chronicled every game for several of those early seasons of the embryonic Penguins.

Bill Heufelder covered hockey for the *Pittsburgh Press*. A native of "Hockey Town" Detroit, his dad was a Red Wings season ticket holder. Bill

The Civic Arena was an architectural marvel when it was built in 1961. It had the first retractable roof built at a major sports venue in the world. It would house, among other things, the Pittsburgh Penguins and their first potential superstar, Michel Brière. Just as his game was going to another level, he was tragically killed in 1971, the result of a car accident. *Photo courtesy of David Finoli.*

earned a degree in journalism at Marquette and took his first newspaper job with the *Dubuque Telegraph-Herald*. A year later, the *Pittsburgh Press*, the town's afternoon daily, needed a hockey beat writer because there were no takers in-house. Hockey was still a minor league sport in Pittsburgh in 1965, and no one on staff was clamoring to cover the Hornets. Especially since you had to cover the always-scheduled Saturday night games—tough on the social life.

Oh, "Heufy" was delighted to take the job. Dubuque was a nice start, but he didn't enjoy writing stories about "how the post office almost ran out of stamps at Christmastime." Moving to Pittsburgh, he was already somewhat familiar with the Hornets. After all, they were the top farm club of his beloved Red Wings. Two years later, he had a lifetime "do you remember where you were?" moment. "I was standing by the teletype machine in the *Press* sports department at the announced-in-advance time, knowing a big decision would be coming off the wire," Bill recalled. That announcement would herald which six cities would be awarded expansion franchises in the big-league NHL. There were more applicants than the half dozen needed. And Buffalo seemed to have an edge over Pittsburgh.

The teletype machine chattered, and the paper flowed. Bingo! Pittsburgh was one of the selected six. "I was a kid in a candy store," Heufelder remembered. "I had a major league beat. Still, no one in the sports department raised an eyebrow. Hockey was nothing anybody really cared about other than the 5,000 or so hard-core Hornets fans."

The first two Pittsburgh Penguins seasons were forgettable flops. The team aptly named for a flightless bird didn't soar on the ice or the box office.

Penguins General Manager Jack Riley felt he had no choice but to try to win right away. The Hornets had gone out in style, winning the 1967 Calder Cup. Many fans wanted the new team to pick up the name of the nasty insect, but Riley's expansion team was stuck with a moniker he hated because "a Penguin is a bird that doesn't fly and is kind of a fat, wobbly one at that," he would admit later. "But that's what you get when one of the owners' wives submitted the name and then, of course, that name won the name-the-team contest with the fans."

With a "win right away" mentality related to following the successful Hornets, Riley drafted a lot of players who had played in the NHL. Some, like Leo Boivin and Andy Bathgate, would eventually be Hall of Famers— but not because of their exploits in Pittsburgh. Add the injuries to key players like Earl Ingarfield and to a lack of depth with no farm system as yet, and not only did the Penguins flounder, but they also didn't even make the playoffs the first two seasons under Coach Red Sullivan.

The ownership group did not have deep pockets, and the franchise was in the red financially and already a candidate to vacate Pittsburgh. But along came another "Red," Leonard Patrick "Red" Kelly, who replaced Sullivan, and some fresh faces, thanks to some deft moves by GM Riley. The general manager had begun the youth movement going into the second season when he traded the team's number one draft choice to Boston for a pair of young players, including Jean Pronovost, who would score almost 400 goals in his NHL career. Late that 1968–69 second season, Riley traded Ingarfield, future Pens coach Gene Ubriaco and George Konik to the Oakland Seals, garnering a trio of "badass" tough guys: Bryan Watson, George Swarbrick and Tracy Pratt. The Pens, who some say were "allergic to wood" along the boards where contact was plentiful, were pansies no more.

Riley kept adding. He was a former commissioner of the minor league AHL. He knew all the nuances of how to secure players through what the

NHL termed the "reverse draft," where teams would have to expose fairly valuable players who didn't make their "protected list." Through the summer going into the third season, he obtained veteran wingers Dean Prentice from Detroit and Glen Sather from Boston. Prentice would lead the Pens in scoring, and the feisty Sather added to the team's toughness. And Riley purchased the contract of another tough customer, center Bryan Hextall (whose son became a future Pittsburgh GM) from minor league Vancouver and also obtained Ron Schock in a trade from St. Louis.

But it was Brière, that third-round amateur pick, who turned out to be the biggest surprise from the smallest frame. The slightly built 155-pounder from a gold mine community in rugged western Quebec arrived in training camp in Branford, Ontario, with no fanfare. Heufelder and the handful of reporters covering the camp hardly noticed him. But Riley and Kelly knew. The Irishmen got early glimpses of what Brière could bring.

First, Brière tried to coax a few more signing dollars from the GM. "It's not really that much extra money because I'll be playing for the Penguins for the next 20 years," Riley remembered Brière pleading. And new coach Kelly, a Hall of Fame player in his own right, eyed something a lot bigger than the slightly built rookie's physical stature. "Red saw his potential right away," said Ken Carson, the Pens trainer in the early years. "He was a little guy but he had great moves and vision. I remember a preseason game when he made a move on Noel Picard, a really good defenseman, and 'Mike' went right around him. On the bench, we just looked at each other like, 'Did you see that, fellows?' He was smooth."

Brière started his first and only season trying to work his way into more playing minutes. He was "O for October," but he scored his first NHL goal on November 1, 1969, while centering a line with Prentice and longtime Pens winger (and future coach) Ken Schinkel. A YouTube video captures the goal and Schinkel fishing the puck out of the net behind Minnesota North Star goalie Ken Broderick. That line accounted for three of six goals in a 6–3 win at the Pittsburgh Civic Arena.

Brière's regular season stats were modest: 12 goals and a team-leading 32 assists. It was in the playoffs that he showed what he could do and, to Pens fans, showed what they would be missing for many seasons to come.

In the Pens' very first franchise playoff round, Brière scored in overtime to secure a four-game sweep on the road against the Oakland Seals. He had assisted on Bob Woytowich's goal in the third period to force overtime. In the dramatic and fight-filled next round against the Blues, the semifinals, he scored game winners in games three and four to help tie the series at two wins each. He then scored the go-ahead goal late in game six. But during the fairy tale ending of what would be his last game, on April 30, the Blues roared back to win 4–3 on late goals to take the series in six games. In the 10 playoff games in the spring of 1970, he had five goals and three assists to lead all Pens scorers.

Just 15 days later, after returning to his Quebec hometown, Brière was driving his Mercury Cougar sports car when he missed negotiating a curve, crashed and was thrown free from the vehicle, 70 miles from his home. A series of brain surgeries were unsuccessful, and Brière succumbed to his injuries almost a year later, on April 13, 1971. Nine days before that, the Pens had completed a disastrous fourth season, finishing sixth out of seven teams in the NHL West Division and well out of the playoffs.

Brière was absent that season but still present to the team in a tangible way. Carson hung his No. 21 jersey in the Pens locker room for every game that following season. "We really knew he'd never come back but we wanted to make sure no one would ever forget him," remembered Carson, who never handed out a new No. 21 again, a tradition the team honored going forward.

"We'll never know," said beat writer Heufelder. "Bobby Clarke, who came into the NHL the same year, said Brière would have been a superstar. Brière and Clark had almost identical numbers their same rookie year. The early Penguins could have used the boost. They just weren't a big enough part of the Pittsburgh sports scene yet.

"In fact, I remember when Michel died, Jack Riley, who became a great friend, told me two weeks later that he was disappointed I didn't write a column in The Press about his death," Heufelder continued. "It really didn't occur to the sports department. The Pens just weren't important enough then to people."

Before the calendar rolled into the 1980s, the Pens would win but two more playoff rounds in that decade. Michel Brière would plainly still have been in his prime then and for years after. The 1970s were great for Pittsburgh sports, but the Pens played a paltry part in that "City of Champions" nickname Pittsburgh enjoyed. The Penguins would have to wait until the 1990s for their banner waving, and it would begin with another youngster from Quebec province, an 18-year-old by the name of Mario Lemieux. Gretzky, who wore No. 99, was from Brantford, Ontario, and attended Penguins practices and preseason games there as that was the site of Pittsburgh's training camp when he was a youth. In tribute to Gretzky's 99, Mario wore 66.

By 2022, the Penguins franchise had retired only two numbers: first, No. 66, to recognize Mario's greatness, and second, No. 21, so that people would never forget the young star whose jersey number also represented the sum total of years in his lifespan. Would Brière, who would have been 35, played with Lemieux when the latter debuted in 1984?

"Unfulfilled promise, that's what it was," Heufelder said. "Bobby Clarke became a Hall of Famer and like Mario, a two-time Stanley Cup champion in Philly. It's not hard to imagine what Brière would have done. He was good and going to be great."

The 1970s was a great decade for most Pittsburgh sports. For Penguin fans, though, there was more to mourn than to celebrate.

CHAPTER 5

1971: BIG THINGS ACHIEVED

THE 1971 WORLD CHAMPION PITTSBURGH PIRATES

By Frank Garland

Big things were expected of the 1971 Pittsburgh Pirates.

And why not?

Veteran manager Danny Murtaugh's club won the National League East Division title the previous year, getting hot down the stretch to finish 89–73. That was good enough for a five-game advantage over the Chicago Cubs.

And even though the Bucs lost three straight to the Cincinnati Reds in the 1970 National League Championship Series, there was lots to like about the Pirates on the eve of the 1971 season opener.

That fact wasn't lost on the local media; veteran baseball writer Charley Feeney of the *Pittsburgh Post-Gazette* noted that if the Pirates didn't win, "Pittsburgh is going to be full of disappointed fans and some may blame Murtaugh, the 1970 manager of the year."

The unflappable Murtaugh was unfazed. "Being the favorite doesn't bother me," he told Feeney. "But I've been around this game long enough to know nothing is ever won in April."

The Bucs had plenty of familiar faces; veteran right fielder Roberto Clemente was starting his 17th season and remained one of the game's top players. Second baseman Bill Mazeroski, the 1960 World Series hero, earned the Opening Day start at second base. Youngsters Bob Robertson, Al Oliver, Richie Hebner and Manny Sanguillen, who would make up the core of a club that would contend on an annual basis for several more years, also were starters when the 1971 campaign opened.

For all their firepower, the Pirates did not come out of the gates with guns a-blazin'. They finished the month of April at 12–10 and in third place, 1½ games off the pace in the NL East. They picked up that pace in May and found themselves with a 29–19 mark after Memorial Day. But they were still looking up at first place, 2½ games back.

The 1971 Pittsburgh Pirates were a talented team as they captured the franchise's fourth World Series title. Perhaps their most talented player was left fielder Willie Stargell. Stargell led the league with 48 home runs and knocked in 125 runs during that memorable campaign. *Photo courtesy of the Pittsburgh Pirates.*

It wasn't until June 10, on the strength of a Steve Blass's complete game 3–1 victory over the St. Louis Cardinals, that the Pirates moved into first place for keeps. Still, they had their hands full through the month of June, as they clung to a narrow two-game lead heading into July—despite already being 20 games over .500.

The Bucs eventually built their lead to 11 games by late July, only to see it shrink to 3½ games by mid-August. But it never got smaller, and they finished the regular season with a 97–65 record and a seven-game advantage over St. Louis.

That set the Pirates up for their second straight trip to the NLCS, where their opponent would be the San Francisco Giants, who captured the NL West crown by a single game over the rival Los Angeles Dodgers. While the Pirates lineup boasted the aforementioned Clemente, Oliver, Sanguillen and slugger Willie Stargell, among others, the Giants had their share of offensive threats, led by future Hall of Famers Willie Mays and Willie McCovey.

San Francisco's pitching staff also boasted a pair of arms that would find their way to Cooperstown in Gaylord Perry and Juan Marichal. The latter went 18–11 with a 2.94 ERA and 18 complete games in 279 innings. Perry, who finished 14 starts, posted a 16–12 mark with a 2.76 ERA.

While the Giants had to scratch and claw their way into the NLCS, the Pirates were able to relax. But that didn't seem to matter once the series started, as San Francisco posted a 5–4 win in Game 1. The Pirates outhit the Giants 9–7 and led 2–1 going into the bottom of the fifth, when Tito Fuentes and McCovey both touched Blass for two-out, two-run homers, vaulting the Giants in front 5–2, and they held on for a 5–4 win.

Coming to the plate is Pirate superstar Roberto Clemente. He led the team to the 1971 world championship by hitting .341 during the season. In the series, he hit .414 with two clutch home runs while capturing the series MVP. *Photo courtesy of the Pittsburgh Pirates.*

Blass, coming off an injury-plagued 1970 season, had gone 15–8 with a 2.85 ERA during the '71 regular season but mistakenly believed he needed to change his approach in the NLCS.

"I fell into a trap," he said 51 years later. "I'd never been in postseason play before and I felt I had to be a different pitcher because the playoffs are a different level than the regular season. I thought I had to throw harder and strike out more people. But that was a trap. And I got crushed in two starts in the playoffs."

"Crushed" is an apt description. In two starts, Blass yielded 14 hits and 10 runs, 9 of which were earned, in seven innings. In the second of those starts—the decisive Game 4—Blass lasted just two innings, and the Pirates trailed 5–2 when he departed.

In that series-clinching win, Hebner struck a huge blow with a three-run homer in the bottom of the second, and the immortal Clemente's run-scoring single in the sixth proved to be the game winner in what was ultimately a 9–5 victory.

Blass would more than redeem himself in the World Series, when the Bucs moved on to meet the powerful Baltimore Orioles. The O's wasted little time showing the skills that enabled them to win 101 games and breeze to the AL East title, taking the first 2 games at home, 5–3 and 11–3. That left it up to Blass in Game 3 to keep his club alive. After his NLCS beatings, Blass said he "had a little meeting with myself. I told myself, 'I'm not a strikeout guy.'" Instead, Blass reverted to the form that he'd shown during the regular season, and his complete-game three-hit gem cut the Orioles' series lead to 2–1 as the Pirates prevailed 5–1. The win ended the Orioles' 16-game winning streak dating back to the regular season.

"I don't know how," Blass said decades later. "But I pitched the game of my life."

The Pirates followed with two more wins and took a 3–2 series lead into Game 6 in Baltimore. Pirates right-hander Bob Moose got the start, and he gave his club five solid innings of four-hit, one-run ball, exiting with a 2–1 lead. But the usually reliable Dave Giusti surrendered a game-tying single to Davey Johnson in the seventh, and in the bottom of the 10th, Brooks Robinson delivered a sacrifice fly to score Frank Robinson and tie the series at 3–3.

"As soon as (Frank) Robinson slid home under Sanguillen's tag, Murtaugh tapped me on the shoulder and said, 'Tag—you're it,'" Blass recalled.

Indeed, that meant Blass would take the hill for the Pirates in Game 7— not that he was looking forward to it. "A lot of people were rooting hard for Bob Moose in Game 6," Blass said. "But no one was rooting harder for Moose than I was. I had my moment in the sun in Game 3. I didn't need to pitch again—and I wanted Bob to have his moment."

That wasn't meant to be, though, and Blass endured a long and sleepless night prior to Game 7. He got out of bed at three o'clock in the morning and walked the streets outside his Baltimore hotel room. "Imagine if a Baltimore cop had come up to me and asked me what I was doing, and I told him, 'I can't sleep—I'm pitching the seventh game of the World Series tomorrow against the Baltimore Orioles.' I'd still be in a mental hospital somewhere in Baltimore, Maryland."

The morning dragged on before Blass finally made it to Memorial Stadium. But even after warming up, he was a nervous wreck, and he walked the first batter he faced. He was still trying to settle down when Orioles manager Earl Weaver decided to play mind games with Blass, coming out and complaining to home plate umpire Nestor Chylak that the Bucco hurler was in violation of rule 8.01—he wasn't in contact with the pitching rubber when releasing his pitches.

"It was all nonsense," Blass said. "But I got so pissed off, I forgot I was nervous. And then I was able to get into a zone."

All he did after that was pitch the game of his life—again. He allowed only four hits and one more walk while striking out five in a masterful complete-game performance—his second of the series. Clemente, who would be voted the Series' most valuable player, hit a solo home run in the fourth, and José Pagán delivered what proved to be the deciding run when he doubled home Stargell in the top of the eighth to make it 2–0.

Blass surrendered back-to-back singles to Elrod Hendricks and Mark Belanger leading off the bottom of the eighth, and Hendricks scored on a fielder's choice. But Blass induced Davey Johnson to ground out to end the eighth, then retired the side in order in the bottom of the ninth. The final out came when Merv Rettenmund hit a bouncer over the mound to shortstop Jackie Hernández, and Hernández's throw from behind second base to first baseman Bob Robertson retired Rettenmund and ignited a wild celebration by Blass and his teammates.

Blass recalls the moment when Robertson squeezed Hernández's throw at first and clinched the Pirates' fourth World Series championship—and the first since 1960. "I went nuts," he said. "I remember running over to Robertson and saying, 'It's forever. This is what you dreamed about. It's forever.'"

Another of Blass's lasting memories came on the team plane as the group was preparing to fly back to Pittsburgh. Clemente and his wife, Vera, were seated ahead of Blass and his wife, Karen. Clemente walked down the aisle and stopped in front of Blass's row. "He's standing in the aisle and says, 'Come here, Blass, let me embrace you,'" Blass said. "I would have climbed over six elephants to get to him. Neither one of us said a word. We just hugged one another."

CHAPTER 6

1971: AND AN AMATEUR SHALL LEAD THEM...ALMOST

JIM SIMONS AND THE 1971 U.S. OPEN

By David Finoli

This wasn't the way the Jim Simons story was supposed to end. The Western Pennsylvania golfer, born in Pittsburgh and raised in Butler, Pennsylvania, for a short period of time in 1971 made local golf fans forget about their hero Arnold Palmer. After the third round of the U.S. Open, the 21-year-old was threatening to become the first amateur since 1933 to win golf's most prestigious tournament with a two-stroke lead over Lee Trevino. He, unfortunately, didn't hang on, but great things were projected for him. While he had a decent career in golf, it wasn't a Hall of Fame one, and his life, sadly, was also filled with many obstacles. He suffered from fibromyalgia and poor eyesight, as well as drug and alcohol dependency. He owned a hot tub that kept the water extremely warm in an attempt to keep the pain from his malady at bay. On December 8, 2005, he was expected at an evening meeting of men from the Southpoint Community Church. He never showed up, and when his friends went to check up on him at his house, they found him dead in the hot tub. Many thought his addiction to painkillers was a thing of the past. It was not. Investigators found that the drugs he had taken coupled with the heat of the hot tub had most likely caused his heart to seize. This local golf hero was dead at the age of 55.

It was 34 years earlier when the Jim Simons story began to unfold. At 17, he qualified for his first U.S. Open, beating out seven other golfers in five

Arnold Palmer is without a doubt the greatest golfer ever produced in Western Pennsylvania. In the 1971 U.S. Open, though, he was overshadowed by a young amateur from Butler, Pennsylvania, by the name of Jim Simons, who, stunningly, led the open after three rounds. *Photo courtesy of the World Golf Hall of Fame.*

playoff holes for the final spot, the second-youngest person at the time to ever qualify for the event. He shot 25 over that year while missing the cut. A year later, he qualified once again, this time making the cut and getting the opportunity to play with Palmer in the final round. He went to college that fall, the University of Houston, eventually transferring to Palmer's alma mater, Wake Forest, becoming a two-time All American with the Demon Deacons. In 1971, he qualified for his third open, and this time he made headlines, stunning golf fans everywhere with his spectacular play.

The scene was one of the most iconic golf courses in the country, Pennsylvania's second-most-popular U.S. Open golf course, Merion Golf Club in Ardmore. Simons was not a powerful golfer, but the light-hitting 21-year-old made up for his lack of power with accuracy. He had made the cut in his second open three years earlier and would do the same at Merion. Simons shot par each of his first two rounds with matching 71s, but on Saturday he would shoot the round of a lifetime.

The list of golfers within five shots of the lead was Hall of Fame worthy and included Jack Nicklaus (who was embroiled in a controversy with Palmer that stemmed from Arnie's complaint about Jack's slow play), Lee Trevino,

Chi-Chi Rodriguez, Ray Floyd and Palmer himself. They all stood behind an amateur, though, as Simons shot a spectacular 65 in the third round to hold a two-stroke lead over the great Nicklaus.

After shooting a 32 on the front nine, Simons continued to impress on the back nine, including the last five holes of the round, arguably the toughest stretch on the Merion East Course, the highlight of which was when he saved par on 14 with a spectacular chip from the heavy rough just off the green. Two holes later, on the difficult 16th, after another great chip that brought his ball to within five feet of the hole, he kicked in a birdie. Several members of Arnie's Army, the enthusiastic group of fans that followed Palmer around the course, broke off to cheer for the man who was becoming a hero to Western Pennsylvania on this afternoon.

While it had been 38 years since an amateur last won a U.S. Open, it was only four years previously when one had the lead after three: Marty Fleckman, who finished the tournament with a horrific 80. The Wake Forest product was very aware of Fleckman and his failed quest for glory. In a column by Bill Lee, sports editor of the *Hartford Courant*, Simons stated, "Sure I know what happened to Fleckman, and I hope it won't happen to me. I've never had a lot of natural confidence, but my maturity and experience have been building over the last two years, especially since playing in three [U.S.] Opens, the Masters, in Walker Cup matches and in the British Amateur [where he was a runner-up earlier in the year]." Luckily, Simons didn't collapse like Fleckman did in 1967, but he wasn't at his best in the final round, either.

Simons told reporters it wasn't a peaceful evening that Saturday night, although he did get some rest. In an article by *Boston Globe* writer Joe Concannon, the young golfer said, "I just tried to rest. I tried to take it easy. I don't think I got eight hours sleep. I woke up a couple of times. I was tossing and turning. I had dinner with my parents at the Holiday Inn and I sat around and watched television."

In the end, he shot a 76 but had a shot to tie Lee Trevino and Jack Nicklaus at 280 on the 18th hole, where he needed a birdie. He was in the rough and tried to get to the green with a wood, but the ball didn't travel far. He ended up with a double bogey, which ended his tournament at 283, in a tie for fifth place, as Trevino would defeat Jack by three strokes in an 18-hole playoff the next day.

Nicklaus was complimentary of the young amateur after the fourth round concluded. "He had a lot of birdie putts that were close but just didn't drop. Jim sets the club perfectly at the top of his swing. He's quiet. Most young players are quick up there. It's a sign of a swing that will last a long time." The Hall of Famer was correct. Simons went on to win three PGA tournaments, including the 1979 Memorial and the 1982 Bing Crosby National Pro-Am. Unfortunately, his life spiraled out of control and, on December 8, 2005, ended in the most tragic of ways.

CHAPTER 7

1972: A CULTURE SHOCK FOR THE AGES

THE 1972 PITTSBURGH STEELERS

By David Finoli

I f there had been social media in the middle part of the 20th century, Art Rooney Sr. would not have been remembered so fondly as the patriarch of the Steelers family. He most likely would have been thought of more along the lines of how current Pittsburgh Pirates owner Bob Nutting is perceived. For the better part of their first 40 seasons of existence, the Pittsburgh Steelers were the embarrassment of the National Football League. They made exactly one postseason appearance, a 21–0 loss at Forbes Field against the Philadelphia Eagles for the Eastern Division championship, and had not one division title to their résumé. Rooney had trouble picking coaches who could take them to the next level, and the draft picks, when they didn't trade them off, were generally huge disappointments, such as 1968 number one draft pick Mike Taylor out of USC; 1956 bonus choice Gary Glick, whom they scouted out of a magazine; or their first-ever pick in 1936 out of Notre Dame, William Shakespeare, who did nothing more for the team than give them a unique name for a trivia question. Even when they got the player right, such as Johnny Unitas or Len Dawson, they traded them away and had to watch their Hall of Fame careers blossom in other cities. To say the Steelers had a losing culture was an understatement.

Art Sr. eventually turned over operations to his son Dan, who hired an unknown assistant coach by the name of Chuck Noll in 1969. Noll was tough and young, but after the Steelers dropped 13 consecutive games following an opening day win against the Lions that season, it didn't look like that

John "Frenchy" Fuqua was a good running back for the Pittsburgh Steelers who held the team record for rushing yards in a game with 218. He was more famous in Steeler lore for being leveled by Jack Tatum on the Immaculate Reception pass as many wonder, even today, "Did it bounce off Frenchy or Tatum?" *Photo courtesy of Morgan State University Athletics.*

losing culture would ever change. The Taylors, Glicks and Shakespeares of the world eventually became draft picks by the name of Joe Greene, Terry Bradshaw, L.C. Greenwood, Mel Blount and Jack Ham as the team seemed to be getting better, winning five games in 1970 and going 6–8 in 1971. Still, we were three years into the Noll era, and the team was still looking at the wrong end of a .500 record in each campaign. In 1972, they drafted a back out of Penn State by the name of Franco Harris. Some in the organization wanted to take Robert Newhouse out of Houston, but Noll stuck to his guns and took Harris. Franco would turn out to be the piece that put the team over the top, as 1972 proved to be the season that the culture finally changed to a winning one—a culture shock for the ages, if you will. By the end of 1972, this franchise finally had the division title it had craved for so long and had transformed into the legendary franchise that it is today.

The Steelers began the year facing off against another young team, the Oakland Raiders. They were underdogs, and it would be a firm test of just how Noll's squad was progressing. By year's end, the Raiders would turn from being just a nondescript opening day opponent into, arguably, their most hated rivals.

The offense had a challenging performance, amassing only 247 yards for the game, but thanks to a blocked punt returned for five yards by Henry Davis for the game's opening touchdown and five turnovers forced by the young Steeler defense, Pittsburgh broke out to a 27–7 lead. What looked like an insurmountable third-quarter lead almost disappeared as Raider QB Daryle Lamonica led Oakland to three fourth-quarter touchdowns, but Pittsburgh held on for the opening day 34–28 victory.

Offensively, the team continued to struggle over the next three weeks, losing two of three contests to go into their week five matchup against the Houston Oilers with a mediocre 2–2 mark. Fans wondered if any progress had been made over the previous two seasons. Enter Franco Harris.

Harris had yet to make any significant mark on the team, to this point amassing only 79 yards rushing in four contests. Against Houston, he would crush his season's output to this point, showing the league this future Hall of Famer's potential. After giving up a touchdown on a blocked punt by the Oilers, Pittsburgh was down 7–0. Harris scored in the second and rambled for 115 yards, with the Steelers easily defeating their division rivals 24–7. The losing ways were about to wash away as the team began to assert the dominance they would become known for over the rest of the decade.

Over the next three weeks, Pittsburgh rolled over New England, Buffalo and Cincinnati by a combined 111–41 score as Harris ran for 111, 138 and 101 yards, respectively. After the young squad turned a 7–0 deficit at the half to a 16–7 win over Kansas City at Three Rivers, the Steelers stood at 7–2, eclipsing 1971's win total, with a date against the hated Cleveland Browns in Cleveland on the horizon. Unfortunately, despite Harris's sixth consecutive 100-yard performance with 136 yards, a Don Cockroft 26-yard fourth quarter ended the team's five-game winning streak with the Browns on top 26–24. How would the Steelers react the following week against the Vikings? Would they fall back or continue the momentum forward toward their bright future?

It was a tight game knotted at 10 in the fourth quarter when Pittsburgh scored the last two touchdowns of the game in a 23–10 victory and a return date against the Browns a week later at Three Rivers Stadium. The young Pittsburgh squad made a statement on that afternoon, crushing Cleveland 30–0 as Franco, for the eighth consecutive time, eclipsed 100 yards and the defense allowed the Browns only 126 yards in this lopsided affair.

At 9–3, the team had their first division title in sight if they could beat Houston and San Diego on the road to end the season. After a 9–3 win in the Astrodome—a game where Harris was held to only 61 yards, although he went over 1,000 yards for the season—they went to face the Chargers with a simple task: defeat San Diego, and the Central Division was theirs. After Bradshaw was tackled in the end zone for a first-quarter safety, cutting their lead to 7–2, the defense took matters into their own hands, limiting the great John Hadl and the Chargers to only 172 yards while forcing seven turnovers in a one-sided 24–2 historic victory that gave Art Rooney and his franchise their long-awaited championship.

Yes, we would have a play called the Immaculate Reception—which we explore in greater detail in chapter 9 of this book—and yes, a fake punt from a well-forgotten punter by the name of Larry Seiple was a key play in a 21–17 loss to the undefeated Miami Dolphins in the AFC Championship game the next weekend, but the future had been set for the Pittsburgh Steelers. The losing days were behind them as a culture shock for the ages came to this team in 1972.

CHAPTER 8

1972: THE ERROR

ON ROBERTO CLEMENTE'S JOURNEY TO REACH 3,000 HITS, I WAS A DAY EARLY AND AN OFFICIAL SCORER'S RULING AWAY FROM SEEING HISTORY

By Chris Fletcher

September 29, 1972. I grabbed my baseball glove and headed to the car with excitement. It was a four-star day. Star one: I was going to a Pirates game at still-sparkly Three Rivers Stadium. Star two: Tom Seaver, perhaps the best pitcher in baseball, was starting for the rival New York Mets. Star three: I was going to see my favorite player, Roberto Clemente, and sitting in right field. Most importantly, star four: Clemente was sitting on hit number 2,999, just 1 away from baseball immortality.

Only 10 other players had reached that magical level, and only 3—Hank Aaron, Willie Mays and Stan Musial—had done so in the latter half of the 20th century. So much was working against him. As the season started—or, more accurately, didn't start, because of a mini strike that wiped out some games—he stood only 118 hits away from 3,000.

Then came the injuries. At 39, Clemente missed a lot of games. At the beginning of the season, I figured that he would reach the mark by the end of July, worst-case scenario mid-August. But as the calendar reached the end of September, it now seemed questionable to some that Clemente would reach 3,000 at all this season. But I refused to believe that. I was 10 going on 11 and a full-fledged baseball junkie and Clemente devotee. And I didn't lose faith.

However, manager Bill Virdon wasn't doing Clemente or me any favors. With the Pirates already having clinched the National League East title,

In 1972, on what turned out to be his last major league regular season at bat, Roberto Clemente joined the 3,000 hit club with a double off the Mets' Jon Matlack. The night before, he thought he had the hit, but it was ruled an error by scorer Luke Quay. *Photo courtesy of the Pittsburgh Pirates.*

Virdon seemed more intent on resting Clemente than having him continue his march on history. I wished Danny Murtaugh were still running things. The Irishman would have made sure of 3,000. But it came down to this: five regular season games remained, and I was going to be at one of them.

After settling in our seats, it didn't take long. In the bottom of the first, Clemente tapped a bouncing ball up the middle. Second baseman Ken Boswell tried to field the grounder, but the ball caromed off his usually reliable glove. The message on the scoreboard at Three Rivers Stadium almost immediately flashed "H"—number 3,000! The crowd of more than 24,000 fans erupted.

I looked up at scoreboard, and moments later, much to my dismay, the scoreboard flashed another message: "E." The official scorer, Luke Quay, a writer and editor for the now-defunct *McKeesport Daily News*, had apparently ruled the play an error from the outset. But in the pandemonium, nobody heard him. He, however, certainly heard the boos of the crowd. On the field, first base umpire John Kibler had already presented Clemente with the ball. Like the fans, Clemente was also disappointed and angry.

I brushed it off. There was still a game to be played, and Clemente would get at least another three shots at Seaver. Tom Terrific and Pirates starter Nellie Briles were locked in a scoreless pitchers' duel. Next time up, Clemente led off the fourth and was caught looking. Ugh, I thought it was a ball, but sitting in right field, my view was probably not as good as the home plate umpire's. Seaver was dealing and painting the corners. In the sixth, Clemente grounded weakly to first.

In the top of the ninth, the Mets finally broke through. Wayne Garrett led off the inning with a double and scored on a single by former World Series hero Tommy Agee. It was the only blemish on Briles's night. There was hope, though. Clemente was leading off the bottom of the inning. I still wasn't worried. Even in the pre-analytics days of baseball, I knew Clemente was a great late-inning clutch hitter, particularly when the Bucs were behind. Some 50 years later, I would learn that he led all batters in the '60s with a .350 average when his team was ahead by a run or tied or the potential tying run was on deck in the seventh inning or later. Hank Aaron was next at a very distant .327. Thank you, Bill James, for that gem.

However, on this day, Seaver was in command. Clemente hit a routine fly ball to right, ending my chance to see 3,000 in person. Willie Stargell and Al Oliver struck out to end the game, giving Seaver a masterful 1–0 shutout. Walking down the ramp as we left the stadium, I tried to justify my disappointment over the official scorer's call. It was an error, I reasoned. Boswell was normally a pretty good fielder, according to my Strat-O-Matic game. Plus, it wouldn't be right for 3,000 to come that way. It needed to be a no-doubter, one that showcased the Great One's batting prowess.

Reaching the parking lot, I was ready to move on in the chase. One of the joys of baseball—even for a fan—is that much like life, you put the day's game behind you and get ready for the next. No dwelling, just moving forward to tomorrow and the opportunities it brings.

Unfortunately, I wasn't going to be there in person for that tomorrow. Instead, I would have to follow the words of Pirates announcer Bob Prince on my transistor radio. These were the days of home games being blacked out on local TV. And the thought of being able to get a cable package that provided access to every baseball game every day wasn't even an imaginable fantasy. In some ways, the crackle and hiss of the AM transistor radio made you appreciate the TV broadcasts more when you were able to see your team.

On September 30, I had the Gunner at my side, his tinny voice emerging from my well-worn Realistic radio with the somewhat mangled antenna that didn't extend all the way. Thankfully, KDKA broadcasted with a gazillion watts, so I could get pretty good reception in Patterson Township even with half an antenna.

Clemente was in the starting lineup. Thank you, Virdon! He would be facing lefty rookie phenom Jon Matlack. I liked the matchup. Matlack made a lot of hitters go fishing after bad pitches. Clemente feasted on hitting pitches out of the strike zone. That's what made him so infuriating for opposing hurlers.

Matlack fooled him in the first, striking him out. But by the fourth, Clemente was clearly ready for the chase to end. He laced a double to the gap against Matlack to begin the inning. This was no dribbler. It was pure Clemente, crushed to the opposite field. You couldn't write the script any better.

That night, on the evening news, I saw the clip. I was disappointed not to have been there and that only 13,000 fans had been in attendance. But if I close my eyes, I can still see his pose at second base, head slightly cocked back, waving to the crowd. Clemente reached 3,000 on his final at-bat of the regular season. If only I had been there.

CHAPTER 9

1972: TWO DIFFERENT WORLDS

SEEING THE IMMACULATE RECEPTION THROUGH
THE EYES OF DAVID FINOLI AND CHRIS FLETCHER

By David Finoli and Chris Fletcher

For the majority of the Steeler Nation, the Immaculate Reception is seen as the moment the inept Pittsburgh Steeler franchise became a dynasty. It was the first postseason victory in the 40-year history of the franchise on a play that is considered by the league as the greatest one the NFL has ever seen (there was even a vote by the NFL that made it official—really). It's strange, though, how the play is viewed and recalled by the two authors of this chapter, David Finoli and Chris Fletcher. One will tell you that it was the greatest moment of his sports life, so thrilled was he to be in the stadium with over 50,000 fans enjoying it, while the other will tell you how he looked on in frustration as he stood outside the Three Rivers Stadium the moment it happened, hearing the fans roar as loudly as he had ever heard, assuming the Steelers had won, perhaps by a Roy Gerela field goal—but not knowing what he had missed until he got into his father's car across the Fort Duquesne Bridge. A tale of two different worlds, if you will.

Let's first set up the game and how we got to that point before these two differing tales are told. Up to this point in the history of the Pittsburgh Steelers, winning seasons were about as rare as a blizzard in July, and championships were nonexistent. Since 1933, they had been involved in exactly one playoff game, in 1947, when they faced off against the cross-state Philadelphia Eagles after the two tied for the Eastern Division title

Author David Finoli's ticket stub from the famed Immaculate Reception game. Unfortunately, he would never see the play live, as his dad, frustrated by Ken Stabler's touchdown, made them leave the contest before Franco had a chance to make his dramatic catch. *Photo courtesy of David Finoli.*

in the regular season. The Eagles dominated and won the contest 21–0. In the offseason, the coach who led them there, the great Jock Sutherland, died of a brain tumor, thus ending the brief greatest era of the team's history (yes, when your greatest era is one season, you have a troubled franchise).

Dan Rooney took over leading the team from his father, Art, in the late 1960s and made the smart decision to hire Baltimore Colts assistant Chuck Noll to coach the club in 1969. While they finished 1–13 that season, they slowly built the team to respectability with a slew of draft picks that they hoped would end their losing ways. Finally, after getting their franchise running back Franco Harris in the 1972 draft, they took that next step in a big way. Finishing 11–3, they captured their first title of any kind, winning the Central Division. In the first round of the playoffs at Three Rivers Stadium, they would face the Oakland Raiders, a team they defeated there in the season opener 34–28. The offensive fireworks that were seen in that opening contest would not be apparent in what turned out to be a physical defensive affair.

CHRIS CHIMES IN: The funny thing is that I was also at that opening game, my first live NFL game. Thanks to a series of books I bought at the Scholastic Book Fairs, I became a fan of the great players from the now-defunct American Football League. So, the chance to not only catch the Steelers but also see former AFL greats George Blanda and Daryle Lamonica was exciting. But Blanda didn't fare so well and was benched for Lamonica, who almost led the Raiders back from a 27–7 deficit.

I, like most people at the rematch, expected a shootout, but frankly I was excited just to be there. I'm still surprised that I was. My uncle chose to take me to the game instead of his fiancée, which I'm sure caused an interesting discussion. (She would accompany him to the following week's AFC Championship Game, while I listened on the radio.) Also interesting was the person sitting in front of us who somehow managed to smuggle in

PITTSBURGH SPORTS IN THE 1970S

a full-size bullhorn, which he used to berate the Raiders. I can't imagine anyone even attempting such a thing these days. Raiders running back Marv Hubbard became "Mother Hubbard" and then something much worse, which also involved the word "mother."

That scene in the stands was actually more exciting than the game, which was a combination of defensive struggle and offensive ineptitude. This time, Lamonica got the start, but he was awful, throwing two interceptions and compiling a quarterback rating of 2.8. Both teams struggled to move the ball, and the half ended. And on the sideline, quarterback Kenny Stabler, who had also been pulled in the opener, was warming up.

TIME FOR DAVE'S THOUGHTS: After a scoreless first half that didn't exactly keep the fans awake, the second half, for the most part, continued along the same path. The Steelers had seemingly gotten the better of the play in the first two quarters but had nothing to show for it. In the third quarter, Terry Bradshaw changed his strategy from attacking the Raider secondary with the long pass to catching Harris underneath with shorter passes, and he began to move the team. Once Oakland made the adjustment to cover Harris, he went back to the bomb, hitting receiver Ron Shanklin to set up a Roy Gerela 18-yard field goal and giving Pittsburgh its first points of the game and a 3–0 advantage going into the fourth quarter.

Raider quarterback Daryl Lamonica was having a miserable day, and after he tossed his second interception of the day, John Madden replaced him with their hope for the future, Ken Stabler, who initially provided little relief to the Oakland offense. After losing a fumble deep in their own territory, Pittsburgh took advantage once again with a 29-yard Gerela field goal, increasing the Steelers' lead to 6–0. As time was running out in the game, with the Raiders needing a touchdown, all of a sudden, Stabler began reminding people of his Hall of Fame talent.

CHRIS CHIMES IN: It was also about this time that I was bugging my uncle for a Coke. I was thirsty and wanted him to flag down a vendor from a section over. He was incredulous that I would ask at such an important part of the game, when the Steelers were about to wrap things up.

BACK TO DAVE'S THOUGHTS: Doing what no one else had for the better part of the game, Stabler began driving Oakland through the seemingly impenetrable Pittsburgh defense. Completing four passes on the drive (Raider quarterbacks completed only a combined 12 on the day), three of which were on third down, the visitors found themselves deep in Steeler territory at the 30. With time running out, Stabler took the snap as Pittsburgh came in on a safety blitz. Rookie defensive lineman Craig Hanneman, who had just replaced Dwight White, came after the slippery Oakland quarterback. He stated in a *Pittsburgh Press* article, "I put an arm out, but he did a reverse pivot. I was outside because we had a safety blitz going and I closed down. I should have smelled a rat." What Hanneman saw was Stabler roll to his left, where the slow-footed quarterback saw nothing but green turf. He went into the end zone for the touchdown and a 7–6 Raider lead. For forty years, my father, Domenic Finoli, had been a devout Pittsburgh Steelers fan and had been used to nothing but disappointment, so in his head, this was just par for the course. He also hated traffic with a passion. It was at this point that Dave Finoli's and Chris Fletcher's lives took a dramatic turn.

Dad turned to me and my brother Jamie and muttered, "Let's get out of here; at least we can beat traffic." We began our descent from section 617, and as the Pittsburgh offense continued to be ineffective on their final drive, we hit gate C of Three Rivers Stadium, looking toward the long walk over the Fort Duquesne Bridge that we'd have to take to get back to our car and beat that hated traffic. It was then that a sudden roar came up, one louder than any of us had ever heard at a sporting event. It was deafening. Had the impossible happened? Had Roy Gerela kicked a field goal somehow to win the game? When we got to our car, we heard what had happened. The most dramatic play in football history—hell, perhaps in the history of sports itself. There was a depression, of course, over what we had missed, but it was overcome with a joy that they had won and would move on to the AFC championship a week later (that game the Steelers lost to the undefeated Miami Dolphins—and yes, we all stayed for the whole game). Throughout the rest of Dad's life—and it was a long one; he passed away in 2016 at 100 years old—Jamie and I would always kid him about missing the Immaculate Reception. As frustrating a memory as ours might have been, luckily, Chris's experience was better.

Chris chimes in: I still have my program from the game, which has the Coke stain on it from when I spilled my drink as I rose to see the chaos. The truth is that I really didn't have a good look at the play that was going away from us. I felt discouragement when the ball bounced off Jack Tatum (more on that in a second), thinking the Steelers' season had ended as the team would be turning the ball over on downs. But then I heard the cheering and saw Franco running down the sidelines and delivering a hell of a stiff

PITTSBURGH SPORTS IN THE 1970s

arm. And although I didn't realize what was happening in the moment, it was great to be part of NFL history and not standing on a stadium ramp somewhere (sorry, Dave).

I still get asked about being there and what I thought about the most famous—and for some the most controversial—play of all time. Controversial because some thought the ball hit off Frenchy Fuqua and then was caught by Franco, which, according to the rules of the time, would have meant the play was over because two offensive players couldn't touch the ball consecutively. It would be a few years before 11-year-old me would pull down an A in physics class, but I offer this scientific explanation: the ball and Frenchy Fuqua are knocked backward during the impact. According to Newton's Law, Tatum's momentum is transferred to the prone Fuqua and to the ball. Had the ball hit Frenchy, it's doubtful that it would have bounded so far backward toward Bradshaw where the pass originated. It's Tatum's force that is transferred to the ball. Physics says so, and so do I. Maybe we should ask Dave what he saw…oh, wait.

CHAPTER 10

1972: THE WILD PITCH

By Frank Garland

Bob Moose had nearly pulled off an escape of Houdini-esque proportions.

Entering the bottom of the ninth inning of the deciding game of the 1972 National League Championship Series with the score tied 3–3, two runners aboard and a 2–0 count on Cincinnati's César Gerónimo, the Pirates' stout right-hander had retired Gerónimo on a fly ball and induced Darrel Chaney to pop out to shortstop Gene Alley in short left field.

Only Hal McRae stood in the way of Moose getting out of the jam and giving the Pirates a chance to live another inning.

But with the count 1–1, Moose unleashed a slider that was meant to coax McRae into swinging at a pitch out of the zone.

Instead, the slider hit the dirt wide of home plate, bounced past Pirates catcher Manny Sanguillen and rolled to the screen. In the process, George Foster, the Reds' runner at third, raced home with the game-deciding— and the series-deciding—run before a crowd of 41,887 at Cincinnati's Riverfront Stadium.

The 4–3 victory sent the Reds on to the World Series, where they would become the first of the Oakland A's three straight Series victims. The loss ended the Pirates' dreams of winning back-to-back championships and would prove to be the last game ever played by Pirates legend Roberto Clemente, who died in a plane crash on New Year's Eve while bringing supplies from his home in Puerto Rico to earthquake victims in Nicaragua.

Sitting the second row in the middle is pitcher Dave Giusti. While he was one of the best relievers in the game in 1972, unfortunately, he gave up a home run to Johnny Bench in the ninth inning of game five of the NLCS, which tied the score. The Pirates would go on to lose the game and the series later on that inning thanks to a Bob Moose wild pitch. *Photo courtesy of the Pittsburgh Pirates.*

Sanguillen said after the game that Moose's pitch hit something but he didn't know what before it bounced past him.

"I jumped to the ball," Sanguillen told a *Pittsburgh Post-Gazette* reporter. "The ball hit me on my hand and bounced on by."

He never got a glove on it.

Moose, lying on a table in the Pirates clubhouse, said he wasn't trying to throw McRae a strike.

"It just took a bounce and bounced over his head, that's all," he said.

Fifty years later, Pirates' starter Steve Blass, who held the Reds to four hits and two earned runs in his 7⅓ innings of work, tried to explain what happened on Moose's wild pitch. Blass said Moose had one of the best sliders in the National League and he put such spin on the ball that when it hit the dirt, you couldn't predict how it would react. In this case, Sanguillen never had a chance, as the pitch was well outside and in the dirt.

Pirates manager Bill Virdon said he didn't go out of his way to console Moose after his fateful 1–1 pitch.

"He's a professional," Virdon said. "He's no kid. He knows how to handle something like this."

The hits kept coming after the game for the hard-luck Moose, whose prized gray 10-gallon cowboy hat was swiped off his head while he was loading suitcases into the trunk of his car at Greater Pittsburgh International Airport after the club had returned home from Cincinnati.

According to a story in the *Pittsburgh Press*, "A youth in his late teens crept up from behind and snatched from Moose's head the $50 wide-brimmed hat he had worn all season," then sprinted away from a crowd of autograph seekers.

Press reporter Joseph Barsotti wrote that Moose immediately went over to two patrolmen leaning on a police cruiser and asked for help, but one of the officers said they had no authority at the airport and were there merely to escort the team into town. Moose then drove away from the terminal, but not before he ran into a third city police officer, and the two exchanged words.

"I'm sorry they didn't take your jacket too," the officer said to Moose in a loud voice.

Although it was a wild pitch that ultimately decided the outcome, the Pirates' bats played a major role in the series loss. As a team, the Bucs batted just .190 after entering the playoffs as the best-hitting club in baseball.

Only two of the Pirates regulars—Rennie Stennett and Sanguillen—batted above .250 in the five-game series. Willie Stargell, a major force all year, went just 1 for 16. Richie Hebner had just one hit in 12 at-bats before getting two hits in Game 5. Gene Alley was hitless in 16 plate appearances. Al Oliver had only one hit in his last 13 series at-bats.

Virdon wouldn't criticize his club, though. "I think it was good Cincinnati pitching rather than poor hitting by us," he told *Press* reporter Bob Smizik the day after the loss.

While the loss certainly stung, Oliver said in a 2022 interview that no one pointed any fingers at Moose for delivering the wild pitch that brought home the deciding run.

"One thing about those Pirate teams of the 1970s, when we got beat, we just walked off the field, went to the clubhouse, got dressed and it was over," he said. "No one ever blamed another player or looked at another player.

There's not one player on that team I could ever remember saying anything about Bob Moose and the wild pitch.

"That's why we won. We liked each other, we respected each other and it could have happened to any player. I could have made an error to cost us that game. Any of us could have. Those were the things that made our teams unique as opposed to other teams. No excuses—we just got beat."

Oliver said he remembers the end of that game "just like it was yesterday. I was out in center field in the last inning. I was out there counting my World Series check because I just knew we were going back to the World Series. I think with losing, sometimes it's how you lose that has a lot to do with it. We had such a confident team that if we got beat in any form or fashion, there just wasn't any excuse."

Blass said he was so confident the Pirates would win the NLCS and collect a second straight World Series share that he had already lined up a contractor to put in a new concrete driveway at his home in Pittsburgh. But Blass said that in the clubhouse following the Game 5 loss, he called that contractor and told him, "Never mind the concrete—we're going with asphalt."

Some experts have said that the Pirates' 1972 team was even better than the '71 club that won the World Series. The '72 team finished 96–59, had nearly identical home and road splits and after moving into first place in mid-June, remained there for most of the rest of the season, with only a couple of momentary exceptions. By September 14, the club had built a 15-game lead and wound up 11 games in front of the second-place Chicago Cubs.

The '71 Pirates went 97–65, spent more time in first place and built their largest lead at 11 games by July 24. That club wound up with a 7-game cushion over the second-place St. Louis Cardinals and beat the San Francisco Giants in the NLCS before edging the Baltimore Orioles 4 games to 3 in the World Series.

Count Oliver among those who believe the '72 Bucs were the superior squad. "The '72 team was better because we had a set lineup," he said. "When you have guys who play every day, automatically with the talent we had, each one of us was going to be better. When you don't play every day, you're not going to be as good. The set lineup is what made the difference."

Oliver said going into the '72 NLCS, no one on the club feared the Reds. "We were a highly confident team," he said, "and having won in '71 gave us even more confidence. We felt that nobody could beat us."

CHAPTER 11

1973: THE STORY OF BRUNO, CHAMPION ONCE AGAIN

By David Finoli

The truth is, I'm not much of a wrestling fan. Sure, when I was a kid, we all played Studio Wrestling in Pittsburgh, and we all wanted to be Bruno Sammartino. As I got older, the excitement of wrestling faded away, but as I began to write books about Pittsburgh sports history, the research I had come across about Bruno the man proved much more impressive than anything he did inside the ring. Yes, he had two long reigns as a titleholder and is arguably the greatest wrestler ever produced in this country, but his family's struggles during World War II and his stance against steroids in wrestling, which was very unpopular in the business, showed a heroic side that should make Pittsburghers proud to count Bruno Sammartino as one of its most iconic figures.

OK, so let's start by going into the nuts and bolts of Bruno Sammartino's wrestling career. After immigrating from Abruzzo, Italy, with his family to join his father in Pittsburgh, Bruno was molded into a wrestler with the help of Pitt wrestling coach Rex Peery. After making his debut on December 17, 1959, with a pin against Dmitri Grabowski in 19 seconds, Sammartino would get a shot at the title four years later. At 28 years old, he was given the chance to fight for the World Wrestling Heavyweight championship against Buddy Rogers of Camden, New Jersey, at Madison Square Garden (MSG) on May 17, 1963. Bruno was at his best, defeating the champion at 48 minutes of a scheduled 60-minute bout in front of a sold-out crowd of 20,000 excited fans. The victory began a long tenure as champion for the Steel City legend.

He held on to the title for almost eight years—2,803 days, to be exact until he took on Ivan Koloff at MSG. There had been rumors that Sammartino was going to lose his title on this evening as 21,106, a record for the legendary facility, turned out to see if it was so. It took only 14 minutes and 55 seconds for Koloff to beat the champion as the stunned crowd fell silent. In an article in *Newsday*, a fan, Georgiann Orsi, muttered, "The word had gotten around he was going to lose, but it still hurt. I shouldn't be getting excited, I'm pregnant. I still don't believe it." She echoed the feelings of most people there (except for the pregnant part), as the wrestling world was stunned their popular champion had been defeated. While he did capture the International Tag Team championship with Domenic DeNucci later that year, he seemingly had had enough of the World Wide Wrestling Federation (WWWF) and its leader, Vince McMahon Sr., taking a break from the organization over the next two years even though McMahon attempted to coax him back to try to recapture his title. Finally, McMahon ended the stalemate by promising Bruno a percentage of the gate and a reduced workload.

Bruno fought champion Pedro Morales at Shea Stadium to a memorable draw on September 30, 1972, with Morales keeping his belt. Finally, on December 10, 1973, he fought the champion Stan Stasiak, who took the title from Morales earlier in the year, at the Garden, drawing a record crowd of 22,000 for the event. The crowd rose to its feet, thrilled, when Bruno took the title for the second time by pinning Stasiak at the 12:14 mark. He kept the title for three years and eventually retired from the WWWF in 1977.

Bruno came back to the WWF (dropping the "Wide" out of the moniker) in the 1980s before leaving again in 1988, having become highly critical of the outfit for its usage of steroids and the storylines, which, according to Sammartino, had become vulgar. He even refused induction into its Hall of Fame. An article in the Bleacher Report quotes Sammartino as saying in 1991, "I'm hoping some wrestling-minded people will come back into the scene and perhaps start back from basics, get some good-looking athletes, get away from the steroid crap and painted faces."

Unfortunately, that never happened, as his disagreement with the organization lasted 25 years. Finally, by 2013, the WWE had instituted a wellness policy that addressed the drug and steroid issues within the WWF. That was enough for Bruno to drop his refusal to be inducted into the Hall of Fame, and he was given the honor that he deserved as perhaps wrestling's greatest figure and champion.

Now all this is fine and explains why Sammartino is a revered wrestler and figure in his adopted hometown of Pittsburgh, but the story of how he got here still is perhaps the most impressive thing about him.

Bruna was left with his mother and seven siblings in the Abruzzo region of Italy after his father immigrated to Pittsburgh in 1935 when the future star was only four years old, and the family lived in a poverty that only got worse when the Nazis rolled into town.

The Nazis were killing anyone they came into contact with, so Sammartino's mother took the family from their home to the top of the mountain, where they lived outdoors but were safe from the Nazis. Bruno's son Darryl explained the situation in an article on InsideEdition.com: "They lived outside, and he was a very sickly, sickly kid. They were basically starving to death."

Famed Pittsburgh radio voice Larry Richert, who also was the executive producer on a documentary on Bruno's life, went on to say in the article, "Nazis came to their village, took over, and had at one point captured them, lined them up to be executed. His mother took his brother, Paul, sister, Mary, and him under her arms, and said, 'Don't worry. We'll never be hungry again. We'll never be cold again. We'll be in paradise with Jesus.' Just then, they were saved at the last minute by their own villagers who had followed the Germans and killed them right there on the spot."

Sammartino—who suffered with rheumatic fever, with doctors questioning whether he'd survive—never thought of himself as tough. He claimed the tough one was his mother. Darryl went on to say, "My dad would sit on a rock and wonder if she was even coming back. It would take 24 hours to get there, 24 hours back. My grandmother was captured, she was shot and jumped off the truck and still came up with food."

Luckily, they did survive and eventually joined their father in Pittsburgh in 1950. Thirteen years later, Bruno was champion of the world and, in 1973, began his second reign with the championship belt. Through it all, his story inside the ring was nowhere near as impressive as his one of survival during the war—a time that taught him survival and integrity in life, two attributes that make us proud to call Bruno Sammartino our own.

CHAPTER 12

1973: PICKING UP THE PIECES

THE PIRATES ENTERED 1973 MOURNING THE LOSS OF THEIR GREATEST STAR AND HAD TO GRIND THEIR WAY THROUGH A CHALLENGING, DISAPPOINTING SEASON

By Chris Fletcher

Baseball's opening day is a joyous occasion. It's a reunion of sorts, bringing back scorebooks, box scores, ballpark hot dogs, the sounds of bats meeting balls and a notion that for the next six months, you'll be immersed in a sport that is more marathon than sprint. No matter what your team's roster looks like, opening day is one of hope, with each team starting undefeated.

Well, that's usually what it feels like. But on April 6, 1973, at Pittsburgh's Three Rivers Stadium, the mood was empty and hollow. The Pirates were coming off the worst offseason in franchise history. It started with a painful loss in the National League Championship Series against the Reds. The Pirates entered the top of the ninth in the deciding game with a 3–2 lead, just three outs from returning to the Fall Classic. But a hanging palm ball from Dave Giusti and a Bob Moose wild pitch led to a 4–3 walk-off loss. The chance to repeat, with a team that many considered superior to the 1971 championship squad, was gone just like that.

Agonizing, to be sure, for Pirates fans, but it was nothing compared to how the year would end. On December 31, star outfielder and heart of the team Roberto Clemente was tragically killed in a plane crash while on a mercy mission delivering supplies to victims of a devastating earthquake in Managua, Nicaragua. The overloaded plane crashed into the ocean shortly after takeoff. Clemente's body was never found. His teammate Manny

Roberto Clemente was more than just a phenomenal ball player; he was a great human being. While he was trying to make sure supplies reached the people of Nicaragua after a devastating earthquake, his plane went down over the Atlantic Ocean, killing all aboard on New Year's Eve 1972. *Photo courtesy of the Pittsburgh Pirates.*

Sanguillen was distraught and for days dove in the ocean looking for some sign of his friend and mentor.

Four months was not enough time to heal, not for Sanguillen (who found himself starting in right field replacing Clemente instead of in his usual spot behind the plate), not for second-year manager Bill Virdon (who somehow had to pick up the pieces) and not for a legion of Pirates fans. Yet here they were in force. In fact, 51,695 packed the stadium for the Friday afternoon game. It was the largest crowd in the young history of Three Rivers Stadium. Perhaps they were there to catch the somber pregame ceremony honoring Clemente.

Despite the sorrow, there was a game to be played. The Pirates were beginning their quest for a fourth straight division title in a season of change. With Sanguillen moving to right field, it opened a spot for touted catcher Milt May, who as a rookie two years earlier delivered a game-winning hit in the World Series. Another promising youngster, Rennie Stennett, was making a case for supplanting Dave Cash at second. Two other rookies were looking to make their mark: both Richie Zisk and Dave Parker brought big bats, hoping to break into the lineup.

The one constant that seemed to be in place was starting pitcher Steve Blass. The hero of the '71 World Series with two complete games, including the clincher, Blass was even better in '72, posting a career-best 19 wins and a 2.48 ERA. It's an opening day tradition that the team's best pitcher, usually based on his previous year's performance, gets the start.

But Blass labored from the first pitch. By the second, he had already walked three and given up three singles and a double and was down 3–0. When he was sent to an early shower, the Bucs were down 5–0 against Cardinals ace Bob Gibson. Maybe it was the spirit of Clemente, but the Pirates staged a comeback. Behind Al Oliver, Stargell and Gene Clines, the Bucs rallied for a 7–5 win, with newly acquired lefty Jim Rooker picking up the decision. The team celebrated a hard-fought division win.

Unfortunately, the opener foreshadowed the other great loss of the '73 season—Blass. He completely lost his control and command of all his pitches. It wasn't physical. It was mental. And a new condition was born: Steve Blass Disease, when an athlete suddenly and inexplicably loses his ability. It even became part of an episode of *Northern Exposure* decades later.

But in 1973, it was simply a matter of the wheels falling off, both for the pitcher and his team. His control was gone; he walked 84 batters in 88 innings, and his ERA tripled. While the Pirates might have been able to survive the loss of Clemente, losing their ace in such an ignominious way was too much to overcome.

Yet somehow this team managed to stay in the race in a god-awful division. The Sanguillen experiment in right field failed. By June 15, he was back behind the plate, with Zisk taking over the outfield spot. As August began, they found themselves at 51–53 in third place, six games behind the first-place St. Louis Cardinals and two and a half games behind the second-place Chicago Cubs. A month later, the Bucs blanked the Cubs,

One of Clemente's best friends on the team was catcher Manny Sanguillen (35) who was devastated after the loss of his friend. On opening day in 1973, he tried unsuccessfully to replace Clemente in right field. *Photo courtesy of the Pittsburgh Pirates.*

1–0, moving above .500, tied for first place with the Cardinals. The teams were clustered so closely that the last-place Philadelphia Phillies were just six games out of first.

September brought some key divisional matchups, and hoping to shake up his team, general manager Joe Brown fired Virdon and brought back a fixture to serve as skipper. Once more, Danny Murtaugh was called on to work his magic like he had in leading the team to world titles in 1960 and 1971. Brown's gambit seemed to work at first. The Pirates won seven of their first nine games under Murtaugh and moved into sole possession of first place.

But then came a home and away series against the Mets that would decide the division. The teams split the first two at Three Rivers. When the series moved to New York, it marked the Bucs' last gasp. The season turned on the middle game. The Pirates held the lead three times. Each time, the Mets came back to tie them. And Pittsburgh felt the loss of Clemente in extra innings. The slow-footed Zisk was on first with one out in the top of the 13th inning. Pinch-hitter Dave Augustine hit a deep drive to left field that appeared to be headed over the wall, but it landed on top of the wall and took a bizarre bounce right to Met's outfielder Cleon Jones.

Zisk kept running, and Jones relayed the ball to third baseman Wayne Garrett, who fired to catcher Jerry Grote. Zisk, lacking Clemente's speed, was out by a mile. The Mets won in a walk-off in the bottom of the inning. The next day, the Mets completed the sweep with a 10–2 rout. For some reason, Murtaugh sent a clearly ineffective Blass to the mound to oppose Mets ace Tom Seaver.

Even though there were 10 games left in the season, the Pirates were done. They played lackluster ball against the Phillies and Montreal Expos and finished 80–82 in third place and under .500 for the first time since 1968. The Mets would win the division, upset the Reds in the division series and come to within one game of a world series win against the A's.

For the Pirates, 1973 was the only time they finished lower than second in the decade. They showed remarkable resilience for most of the year. They also set the stage for division crowns in '74 and '75. Increased playing time for Zisk and Parker would spawn the Lumber Co. that would be a staple of the decade. Still, fans couldn't help but wonder: What if? What if Clemente hadn't died? What if Blass had pitched like he had before? The Bucs certainly would have had the pieces to compete for a championship. And maybe the Pirates and not the Reds would be considered baseball's best team in the 1970s.

CHAPTER 13

1973: WHO'S ON THIRD?

THE DEATH OF PIE TRAYNOR

By Chris Fletcher

On his death in 1972, many people thought of Pie Traynor as a pitchman or studio wresting commentator. But why wasn't he recognized as one of the greatest players in Pittsburgh Pirates history? I don't know…third base.

> *Lou Costello: What's the guy's name on first base?*
> *Bud Abbott: No. What is on second.*
> *Costello: I'm not asking you who's on second.*
> *Abbott: Who's on first.*
> *Costello: I don't know.*
> *Abbott: He's on third, we're not talking about him.*

When Harold "Pie" Traynor died in March 1972, we actually were talking about him at the school bus stop. One of my friends said to me, "Did you hear that guy from Studio Wrestling died last night?"

Another friend chimed in, "You mean, 'Who can? Amer-I-Can'?" mimicking Traynor's catchphrase as the spokesman for American Plumbing and Heating Co. Just to emphasize his point, he repeated, "Who can? Amer-I-Can!"

Me, fresh off a marathon session of Cadaco's All-Star Baseball Game, where I had managed Traynor in a four-hit game, coolly replied, "No, dumbasses, he was the greatest third baseman ever." They just looked at me.

My friends could be excused. After all, they were 11 and not budding baseball historians. Yet for some reason, Traynor still doesn't get the respect

By the time he retired as a player in 1937, Pie Traynor was considered by many to be the greatest third baseman of all time. He went on to become a Steel City icon after his days with the Bucs were over, with a thriving local career both in commercials and on TV. The city was saddened by his death in 1972. *Photo courtesy of the Pittsburgh Pirates.*

he deserves—especially in his adopted home of Pittsburgh. That's always bothered me. After all, just three years before his death, when Major League Baseball announced its all-time team to celebrate the league's 100-year anniversary, it selected Traynor as the best third baseman in league history. Sure, since then, Mike Schmidt, George Brett, Wade Boggs and Chipper Jones have come along to lay partial claim to that title. It's not a crowded space. Third base is the least represented position in the Baseball Hall of Fame, with Traynor 1 of 14 to be enshrined. So, why isn't he celebrated more? I don't know…third base.

Here are eight pretty good reasons why you should know Pie Traynor.

1. He could hit.

Traynor posted a lifetime batting average of .320, while topping .300 10 times. A solid 6 feet and 180 pounds, Traynor knocked in 100 or more runs seven times and never struck out more than 28 times in one season in 17 years. His best year may have been 1930, batting .366 and knocking in 119 runs.

2. He was an RBI machine—despite not hitting a lot of homers.
Unbelievably, Traynor drove in 1,273 runs while smacking just 58 home runs. In fact, his career high was 12 in 1923—the only season he had double-digit homers. And he was at his best in the clutch. In the 1925 World Series against the Washington Senators, Traynor hit .346 and singled and homered in his first two at bats against Walter Johnson. It was his single with the bases loaded on the last day of the 1927 season that clinched the National League title.

3. He could field.
The great irony is that as a pitchman/studio wrestling commentator, Traynor made more than his share of errors, often bumbling and mispronouncing names and words. But on the diamond, there were few miscues. He was near perfect at the hot corner.

But it wasn't always that way. Traynor's erratic defense—including 64 errors in one season at shortstop—kept him mired in the minors. He worked closely with Hall of Fame infielder Rabbit Maranville, who smoothed the edges off his game and moved him to third base. It was a smart position change. Traynor holds the National League record for career putouts by a third baseman with 2,288. Not bad for a guy who retired in 1937.

4. He anchored the great Pirates squads of the 1920s.
The Pirates of the '20s were highly competitive, capturing two pennants and a World Championship. While they had stars like Paul and Lloyd Waner, Kiki Cuyler and Ray Kremer, it was Traynor who was the lynchpin of one of the most successful decades of Pirates baseball.

5. He later managed the team.
Traynor suffered a freak injury, fracturing his right arm in 1934 when catcher Jimmy Wilson fell on it. With Dr. James Andrews and his pioneering surgical techniques still decades in the future, Traynor never fully healed and was no longer an impact player.

But he still had an outstanding baseball mind and took over as the Pirates' player/manager from 1934 to 1939. He just missed managing the Pirates to the National League pennant in 1938, when Cubs catcher Gabby Hartnett's famed "homer in gloamin" eliminated the Bucs.

Unfortunately, Traynor took a lot of heat for the Pirates' collapse that year. His critics said he rode his team into the ground, rarely resting his regulars. But Traynor was probably his own harshest critic. By the end of the season, he had lost 20 pounds, was smoking constantly and was said to generally look worn out. It would be years before the Pirates seriously contended again.

6. If it weren't for him, the Pirates might not have signed World Series hero Bill Mazeroski.

Even after his playing and managing days ended, Traynor stayed close to the Pirates' organization. He was a fixture at spring training, working with the infielders. He also scouted and ran tryout camps for the franchise. In fact, he played a big role in discovering a future Hall of Fame second baseman, Bill Mazeroski.

"I had been up to Pittsburgh my sophomore, junior and senior years of high school, so the team knew about me," Mazeroski recalled. "But I went to a tryout camp Pie ran for the Pirates in Follansbee, [West Virginia,] and it wasn't long after that I signed with the team. I guess he put in a good word for me with somebody."

7. Speaking of good words, he made wrestling entertaining.

Pittsburgh was a mecca for wrestling in the '50s and '60s. The mats featured such colorful wrestlers as Bruno Sammartino, Jumping Johnny DeFazio, Dominic DeNucci, Tony "the Batman" Geiger and the highly underrated Frank "Carnegie Cop" Holtz, all beaming into living rooms via WIIC's *Studio Wrestling*. Host Bill Cardille and Traynor made it fun for a generation of wrestling-loving Pittsburghers.

8. "Who Can? Amer-I-Can" was pretty damn effective.

American Heating Company became a top sponsor for *Studio Wrestling*, and Traynor performed the live reads during the Saturday night program. Soon, Pittsburghers repeated that advertising slogan, and Traynor was a powerful pitchman. How powerful? Thanks to his delivery of that catchphrase, American Heating Company became one of the region's top suppliers.

That American's success was tied to their pitchman made sense. What's still puzzling, however, is that Traynor wasn't recognized for his success on the diamond a generation earlier. Even the Pirates missed the mark. His No. 20 was retired posthumously on opening day in 1972. It should have been done earlier. Why wasn't it? I don't know…third base.

CHAPTER 14

1973: THE GREATEST ROUND
OF GOLF EVER

JOHNNY MILLER'S 63 AT OAKMONT

By David Finoli

N ow the reality in golf is that an impressive score at one course may not be equal to the same at another. Let's face it, there are 63s and below shot often on the PGA tour, and while it is a very impressive feat no matter where, not all 63s are the same. If Brooks Koepka shoots a 63 at the Muirfield Village Golf Club in Dublin, Ohio, he will get an "atta boy" on ESPN, but it won't be the headline in every newspaper in the country, nor will he make the cover of *Sports Illustrated*. Now when Johnny Miller shoots a 63 in the U.S. Open, on the final round at one of the world's most difficult courses, namely the Oakmont Golf Course right outside of Pittsburgh, then all the above acknowledgements do happen. In fact, we can take this achievement one step further. Miller's incredible performance that day can arguably be called the greatest round of golf ever shot. And the word "arguably" shouldn't even be used.

Why is this round of golf the best ever shot? Let's break it down step by step. First, we will look at the final round he shot. It wasn't as if Johnny Miller was having the tournament of his life going into the final round. He was a respectable two under par after the first two rounds, tied for third place, three shots behind Gary Player, but had a miserable third round where he shot a 76. He found himself six shots down in 12th place behind a Hall of Fame leaderboard that included Player, Jack Nicklaus, Lee Trevino and Arnold Palmer in front of him. The idea of setting the all-time low for

A more open Oakmont Country Club. Between 1983 and 2016, 15,000 trees were removed. The idea was to get the course looking more like it did when it was designed by H.C. Fownes in 1903. *Photo courtesy of David Finoli.*

a major at that point was not in his thought process. Then Miller started off with a blaze of glory, but still, the thought had to be he could finish in the top five, not win the whole damn thing. Here is his famous round in three-hole increments.

Hole	Yards	Par	Miller's Score	Round Score	Total Strokes	Total Score
1	469	4	3	-1	3	+2
2	343	4	3	-2	6	+1
3	425	4	3	-3	9	E

Miller began his historic day with a three iron that took him to within five feet of the hole, where he made his first birdie. He followed that up with a nine to within one foot on the second hole, which he easily put in for birdie number two. On the 425-yard third hole, he gave himself the first challenge of the day by placing his five-iron shot 25 feet away on the lightning-fast Oakmont greens. He nailed the long putt and pulled himself to even after three consecutive birdies. In an article in *Sports Illustrated*, Miller stated, "After I birdied the 3rd hole, I said to myself, 'Son of a gun. I'm even par,' and I thought, 'Well, maybe I've got a chance to get back in the tournament!' I birdied the 4th. I got a little tight. I almost gagged on a couple of putts at the 7th and 8th but the easy birdie at 9 calmed me down."

Hole	Yards	Par	Miller's Score	Round Score	Total Strokes	Total Score
4	549	5	4	-4	13	-1
5	379	4	4	-4	17	-1
6	195	3	3	-4	20	-1

He was in trouble for the first time on four, in the sand, when he hit a magnificent shot to within six inches for birdie number four as he was now under par for the tourney and thoughts of a potential championship were in his head. Miller's string of one-putts came to an end on five and six as perhaps his phenomenal start was grinding down with two consecutive pars on five and six.

Hole	Yards	Par	Miller's Score	Round Score	Total Strokes	Total Score
7	395	4	4	-4	24	-1
8	244	3	4	-3	28	E
9	480	5	4	-4	32	-1

While he wasn't struggling compared to the rest of the field, Miller hit his worst run of the day the next two holes. At the seventh, he hit the green with a four wood but two-putted for par. The eighth was a difficult 244-yard three par. Miller missed the green then three-putted for what would turn out to be his lone bogey of the day. He rebounded with a birdie at the par-five ninth to make the turn at a spectacular 32. After a four-hole birdieless drought, Miller's championship hopes were once again alive.

Hole	Yards	Par	Miller's Score	Round Score	Total Strokes	Total Score
10	462	4	4	-4	36	-1
11	371	4	3	-5	39	-2
12	603	5	4	-6	43	-3

After a two putt for a par at ten, the soon-to-be champion nailed a 14-foot putt at 11 before putting a four iron to within 15 at the 603-yard 12th hole. He hit the birdie putt there to put him at three under for the tourney. A championship was now truly in sight.

Hole	Yards	Par	Miller's Score	Round Score	Total Strokes	Total Score
13	185	3	2	-7	45	-4
14	360	4	4	-7	49	-4
15	453	4	3	-8	52	-5

After putting a four iron to within five feet of the cup at the par three 13th, which he nailed for another birdie, Miller finally pulled in front for the tourney as Schlee bogied the same hole. Miller would two-putt the 14th for par. At 15, he holed a 10-foot putt, and all of a sudden, the all-time record for a major of 63 was now in sight if he came in at par on the final three holes.

Hole	Yards	Par	Miller's Score	Round Score	Total Strokes	Total Score
16	230	3	3	-8	55	-5
17	322	4	4	-8	59	-5
18	456	4	4	-8	63	-5

Miller needed three consecutive pars to capture not only the tournament but also the major scoring record of 63. He had the opportunity to make it even lower but unfortunately two-putted each hole for the three consecutive pars and a 63 on the button. It allowed him to not only make up the six strokes he trailed at the beginning of the round but also win the tournament by one stroke over John Schlee and two in front of Tom Weiskopf and Nicklaus.

While we understand why it was the greatest round ever shot in 1973, why would it still be five decades later? Consider the following facts.

- Even though the score has been equaled 37 times and was beaten at the British Open in 2017 by Branden Grace, who shot a 62, let's look at these contenders. The U.S. Open is traditionally where the golf course is set up to be the most challenging. The PGA Championship is set up the most like a normal event, while the British Open, though it can be equally as difficult with the weather and wind that usually comes with it, when the weather is mild and the winds low, it's probably the easiest of the four majors to post a great score. The Masters is tough, but at the same golf course yearly so easier for a golfer to get to know. Therefore, out of all these scores, a 63 at the U.S. Open is a much more impressive score.

- Out of the 63s that were shot at the U.S. Open, shooting it in the final round is a much tougher achievement. Those golfers who have shot a final-round 63 in the open include Miller and Tommy Fleetwood in 2018, with Fleetwood finishing second. But Miller doing it in the final round and overcoming a six-stroke deficit to win gives him the greatest round ever.

- He was consistent shooting a 32 on the front nine and 31 on the back nine.

- It wasn't a great weather day. While Lanny Wadkins had a 65, only Schlee, Weiskopf, Nicklaus and Trevino had subpar scores this day.

- He *won* the most difficult tourney in the world with his 63.

- It was at Oakmont—the third-most-difficult course in the country.

- I repeat, it was a 63 at *Oakmont*!

Yes, there are other golfers who should be proud of their achievements in majors, but when it comes to who had the most impressive round at a major, the argument begins and ends with Johnny Miller's spectacular round in 1973.

CHAPTER 15

1973: DOES ANYONE WANT THIS JOB? JOHNNY MAJORS DOES!

By David Finoli

I t had been 36 years since Pitt was consistently a national championship contender, and by 1973, the only thing it was contending for was the worst program in the country. It had been turned down by local wunderkind coach Frank Kush and had trouble convincing anyone why coming to Pitt would be anything more than an exercise in futility. Finishing with a miserable 1–10 campaign, the Carl DePasqua era was now coming to a merciful end. Pitt had to decide at this point whether it would continue to play football at the highest level or drop it to minor status, where perhaps it could compete. They would take one more shot in 1973, and the school finally promised to support it financially. While it seemingly was having trouble convincing any worthwhile candidate that things would be different this time, miraculously, one promising young coach was listening, the man who led Iowa State out of the doldrums to a bowl game. His name was Johnny Majors.

When the university tried to make a splash hire following the less-than-stellar Dave Hart era, where the team went 1–9 each season between 1966 and 1968, new athletic director Casimir Myslinski had to deal with not only a committee that would help pick the new coach but also a concoction called the Big Four, which included Pitt, Penn State, West Virginia and Syracuse—which, among other things, had pledged to limit scholarships and make the academic requirements tougher for incoming players than those of the schools they were competing against. Cas thought he had Windber,

Signing a helmet is legendary Pitt coach Johnny Majors. When it looked like no one wanted the job after a disastrous 1972 campaign, Majors, who was an up-and-coming coach at Iowa State at the time, took on the challenge, eventually leading the program to its ninth national championship in 1976. *Photo courtesy of David Finoli.*

Pennsylvania native Frank Kush, who was doing an incredible job building the Arizona State program, but after initially agreeing to come home, Kush backed off and remained with the Sun Devils, where he continued his Hall of Fame career. Many names were brought up, and all turned the Panthers down, as it was becoming clear no experienced coach in his right mind would want to take over the Pitt program under such restrictions. It was a recipe for disaster, as DePasqua soon found out. After a 1–10 campaign in 1972, his tenure was done at the school. Pitt was back at square one, and the same question had to be answered again: does anyone want this job?!

Many coaches had been mentioned in the process, including the man who had jilted them the first time, Frank Kush, and none seemed to be interested in what the Panther brass had to offer; except for one man—a coach who, surprisingly, had been one of the hottest names on the market, as his name was mentioned seemingly for every job opening in the country. While no one seemed to be taken with what Pitt was selling, Iowa State's Johnny Majors reportedly was very enamored with what would be an epic challenge.

With Kush making the claim that there was no way Pitt could be an instant winner and the other name being mentioned, Homer Smith, the athletic director at North Carolina, not interested either, Myslinski had work to do if he was to convince Majors that Pitt was the place for him.

First off, this time around, Cas would not have to deal with a committee to choose the program's next head coach. It would be his call. He then took Pitt out of the Big Four and worked with school officials to end the language requirement that Panther athletes were subject to for admission to the school as well as making Pitt a much friendlier place for athletes to gain admission to by ending several other admission requirements for them. He also was able to increase their offer to $35,000 a year plus money from a weekly television show the new coach would have. The base pay would be among the most lucrative in the country at the time and $10,000 more than DePasqua received. The enhancements were all fine, but bottom line Michigan State had already interviewed Majors, the former Heisman Trophy runner-up at Tennessee, and there was a chance they might move in and hire the Iowa State coach before Myslinski had a chance to talk to him.

A week after the interview, the Spartans still hadn't made up their mind, and the Pitt athletic director had a chance to sell Johnny on the potential of the program. With all the enhancements he would be given that weren't afforded his predecessors, Majors now was very enamored with the challenge Cas had set in front of him. Soon the rumors were growing that the Iowa State coach had made a decision. The *Knoxville New Sentinel* was reporting that "John Majors, it now appears, is going to Pittsburgh as the new coach of the downtrodden Panthers." The *Atlanta Constitution* said that Majors had in fact accepted the job and signed a lucrative long-term contract.

It was still all unofficial, so Panther fans, who had become so used to disappointment, were holding their breath hoping that it was true. Luckily, it was, and even though there was the thought in their heads that he might back out, as Kush had four years earlier, he did not. He came to the press conference enthusiastic. While promising there would be no instant miracles, he said, "We sure didn't come here to lose."

Majors not only proved Kush wrong by making Pitt instant winners in his first season as they improved to 6–5–1, but by 1976, he'd also made the miracle complete with a 12–0–0 season and the program's ninth national championship. For years, Pitt fans wondered if anyone really wanted the job as head coach of the program. On this day, luckily, someone did.

CHAPTER 16

1973: ON PAR WITH ARNIE

CAROL SEMPLE (THOMPSON) WINS THE U.S. WOMEN'S AMATEUR

By David Finoli

For years, Arnold Palmer dominated the headlines when it came to golf in Western Pennsylvania. He was truly the leader when it came to the sport in the area, and no one was even a close second. In 1973, an amateur golfer from Sewickley put her name in the same rarified air as the Latrobe, Pennsylvania native when she became the first Western Pennsylvanian to capture the United States Women's Amateur championship—a moment that was the beginning of one of the most legendary amateur careers in all of women's golf.

We now know this golfer as Carol Semple Thompson, but in 1973, it would be seven more years before she met her future husband Dick Thompson, so for the sake of accuracy, we will just call her Carol Semple. There, of course, were many national honors and achievements in her future at this point, though she was only known as an accomplished golfer in Western Pennsylvania circles.

Semple came from a golf family: her mother, Phyllis, was a USGA committee woman who went to the quarterfinals of the 1963 U.S. Women's Amateur, and her father, Horton, was a USGA president. In an interview on USGA.org, Semple confided that her illustrious career "means everything because I grew up as a USGA brat." She would beat her mother for her first Western Pennsylvania golf championship in 1964 when she was only 16.

Looking at her trophies is perhaps the most decorated female amateur golfer of all time, Carol Semple-Thompson. In 1973, she became the first person from Western Pennsylvania to capture the U.S. Women's Amateur title. *Picture courtesy of the World Golf Hall of Fame.*

Her main accomplishment by the time the U.S. Women's Amateur began in 1973 was four Western Pennsylvanian titles and a ninth-place finish in the U.S. Women's Open earlier in the year. No woman from the area had ever won the premier event of women's amateur golf. She had reached the quarterfinals, where she was facing the defending champion, Mary Budke. Remarkably, Semple upset Budke 2-and-1 to gain access to the semifinals against Michigan's Bonnie Lauer.

It was there that the Sewickley native showed her grit as she found herself down two to Lauer with three holes left. After an eight-foot birdie putt on

16, which brought her to within one, she parred 17 to tie the match going into the final hole. On 18, Semple chipped a 30-foot shot that came to within four inches of the hole. She completed the par as Lauer stood only six feet away to tie the match and send it into extra holes. Remarkably, Lauer missed the shot as Semple completed the incredible comeback to win 1-up. In the final, she would face Seattle's Anne Quast Sander, who comfortably beat Donna Horton 4-and-3 in her semifinals matchup.

Sander was 11 years Semple's senior and had a much more accomplished amateur career at that point, winning three U.S. Amateur titles, in 1958, 1961 and 1963, while finishing runner-up twice in 1965 and 1968. It was obvious that Semple was the underdog in the 36-hole final and after the 18-hole morning round. After being up two holes early on, she found herself 1-down to the three-time champ by the time they finished. Early on in the afternoon round, it looked like Sander was in a great position to capture her fourth crown.

The 24-year-old Pennsylvanian tied the match on the first hole of the second 18 but quickly fell apart, bogeying both the second and third holes and again at number five. The three bogeys in four holes put her decisively down to Sander by three holes with 13 left to play. Semple would have to find her game and do it quickly if she wanted to become the first golfer from Western Pennsylvania to capture a U.S. Women's Amateur crown.

On number seven, she hit a spectacular iron shot to the green and followed it up with another at eight, which gave her victories at each hole to cut Sander's once-dominant lead to a single hole. She birdied the 10th, which dramatically tied the match. Semple bogeyed the next hole to drop one behind again but when her 35-year-old opponent got caught in a sand trap, the dramatic match was even again with only three holes to play. Could Semple raise her game to capture the match, or would the more experienced Sander hold her off? As it turned out, it would be the three-time champion that would falter.

After halving the 16th, Semple parred the 17th, the hole where Sander fell apart. She had a double bogey, which gave the young amateur her first lead since the first hole of the morning round. She followed that up by matching Sander on the 18th and final hole with a par, and history was hers: Western Pennsylvania now had its first U.S. Women's Amateur champion.

Semple's father, Horton, was ecstatic, as he had the honor of presenting her with the trophy. In a *Pittsburgh Press* article, he said, "I'm numb. Among the three of us—Carol, Phyllis and myself—this is something we waited 25 years for, and it took Carol to do it." Carol was ecstatic, too, exclaiming, "I can't believe it. It's fantastic."

As thrilled as she was, she was also drained from the long week and season she had to this point. "I'm going home. I have no more on tap—but I've played seven tournaments in a row."

Semple would return to the game and become a women's amateur icon, capturing the British Amateur a year later to go along with two U.S. Women's Mid-Amateurs, four U.S. Senior Amateurs and twelve appearances in the Curtis Cup, women's amateur golf's version of the Ryder Cup, as well as two as a nonplaying captain. Eventually, she was given the ultimate honor of being elected to the World Golf Hall of Fame in 2008. Her fabulous career had its start on that August day in 1973 when she put her name alongside Arnie's as Western Pennsylvania golfing elite.

CHAPTER 17

1974: THE GREATEST PROFESSIONAL SPORTS DRAFT OF ALL TIME

By Tim Rooney

Bill Nunn, the NFL Hall of Famer, broke a very tense silence and gained the immediate attention of everybody in the room by stating, "I think we can get Stallworth in the fourth round." That well-calculated prediction was perhaps the key moment that produced arguably the greatest draft in the history of the National Football League. Nunn's very perceptive comment allowed expertise and preparation to begin a domino effect. The scene was the Pittsburgh Steeler draft room at Three Rivers Stadium, and the date was January 29, 1974, the first day of a two-day draft event. It is almost unbearable to think that Nunn's projection should have gone unheeded.

Expectations were very high for the Pittsburgh Steelers coming off the 1972 season, when the team had an outstanding 11–3 regular season record and, of course, the Immaculate Reception victory over the Oakland Raiders in the December 23 playoff game. The Steeler 1973 season started very well with the team winning eight of the first nine games and then losing three in a row. That losing streak resulted in a 10–4 record and a tie with Cincinnati, but the Bengals won the division by winning the tiebreaker. The Steelers wild card berth sent them to Oakland for a one-sided 33–14 defeat. Many football fans who read Roy Blount's book *About Three Bricks Shy of a Load*, about the 1973 Steeler season, will remember the book's account of the

When the Steelers had the greatest draft in professional sports history in 1974, they made their third Hall of Fame choice when they drafted John Stallworth in the fourth round. Stallworth went on to set a club record with 537 catches by the time he was done. *Photo courtesy of Alabama A&M athletics.*

ups and downs of that 1973 season. That year, the team's pass defense was exceptional, and perhaps that led to three of the first five picks being on the team's offensive side of the ball in the 1974 NFL draft.

The 1974 NFL draft headquarters were located in New York City's Sheraton New York Times Square Hotel, where team representatives awaited phone calls from their teams to convey their team's selections. Each team had seventeen choices, and there would be a total of 442 picks during the two-day procedure. Ed "Too Tall" Jones from Tennessee State University would be chosen by Dallas as the first overall pick. Dave Casper (2nd round, 45th overall pick), selected by the Raiders, was the only other non-Steeler HOF player chosen in the 1974 draft, and he was selected immediately before the Steelers selected Jack Lambert.

The Steeler draft room was in Steeler offices at Three Rivers Stadium, a classroom-size room converted from a player meeting room. The room featured long tables, chairs and telephones from NFL draft headquarters in New York. A direct telephone line had been installed, which connected to the scouting combine Blesto headquarters, where Jack Butler and his staff were available for consultation. Bulky black binders containing draft-eligible player reports, organized alphabetically, lined the tables; these binders also contained those players' medical data and contact information.

The room's walls supported boards with attached magnetic labels for each college player who was an eligible draft choice. One board supported an overall list by player grade, regardless of position: his college; position; height, weight and speed; test score; team; and the Blesto scouting combined grades. An adjoining wall displayed labels with the same player information, but this one was organized by players' positions and by grade from top to bottom. Another adjoining wall displayed columns headed by the NFL teams, and as a player was drafted, the player card from the overall board was moved to the team that had selected him.

The placement and rankings of those player information cards were the result of extensive player evaluations based on school visits, film evaluations and game observations by Steeler and Blesto combine scouts and Steeler coaches' input based on their film evaluations and school visits to conduct workouts of the top prospects. And finally, the players were ranked after many long days of meetings to discuss them, attribute values to them and rank them accordingly.

Art Rooney Jr., the Steeler vice president in charge of personnel, head coach Chuck Noll and player personnel director Dick Haley were the major players during draft day procedures. Team owner Art Rooney and team president Dan Rooney were present and intensely interested. Team scouts Bill Nunn and Tim Rooney were constantly in consultation with Art Jr. Coach Noll, Steelers assistant coaches Dick Hoak, Dan Radakovich, Lionel Taylor, George Perles, Woody Widenhofer and Bud Carson were ready for their opinions and involved in moving the player information cards as the draft moved forward. Steeler trainer Ralph Berlin was on a direct phone line to video director Bob McCartney, who was representing the Steelers at NFL draft headquarters in New York. It would be Berlin who conveyed the Steeler choices to McCartney, who then would inform NFL personnel of the Steeler choice in each of those seventeen rounds.

That draft, of course, produced five NFL Hall of Famers for the Steelers, but it is very interesting to note that there were four Hall of Famers in that Steeler draft room: Art Rooney, Dan Rooney, Chuck Noll and Bill Nunn.

Bill Nunn had already made an outstanding contribution to the Steeler roster before the 1974 draft. His reports and the willingness of the Steelers to act on those reports were very instrumental in the acquisition of players from the southern Black colleges, now known as the Historically Black Colleges and Universities (HBCUs). Included in that category were Hall of Famer Mel Blount, Frank Lewis, Dwight White, L.C. Greenwood and Joe Gilliam.

SOMETIME PRIOR TO THE 1974 draft, Bill Nunn traveled to Huntsville, Alabama, to join other NFL scouts on the Alabama A&M campus to time John Stallworth. The field was in poor condition, and Stallworth's 40 times were not very good. The NFL scouts moved on to other colleges, but Nunn decided to stay in Huntsville. The next day, he managed to locate a high school field, one more suitable for timing Stallworth. When Stallworth asked Nunn how well he did, Nunn simply told him he did better but did not tell Stallworth what his 40-yard time was. And thus, Stallworth was unable to tell others how well he performed. It was that 40 time—which only Nunn had—that became a major factor in that draft day crisis and drama, a single statement that was so instrumental in the creation of what most people say was the greatest draft in the history of the NFL. Longtime rumors suggest that not only did Nunn have Stallworth's true 40 times, but that he also had in his possession the best and only films of Stallworth's best games.

Standing next to teammate Chuck Cooper (*third from left*) is Bill Nunn (*second from left*). Playing with Cooper at Westinghouse High School, Nunn went on to West Virginia State to continue his basketball career as Cooper joined him for the first semester before eventually coming back home to Duquesne. *Photo courtesy of Duquesne University Athletics.*

Bill Nunn (*far left*) eventually became a renowned sports reporter at the *Pittsburgh Courier* before becoming an assistant personnel director with the Pittsburgh Steelers. He became one of the major architects of the Steeler Dynasty, scouting talent in the traditional Black colleges at a time when the NFL teams weren't paying proper attention. He eventually was elected to the Pro Football Hall of Fame in 2021. *Photo courtesy of Duquesne University Athletics.*

Eight draft choices and three free agents made the Steeler 1974 roster. The 1974 season saw a significant rookie advantage. The short-lived World Football League signed players, and a training camp strike by veterans picketing the training camps—with their "No Freedom, No Football" signs prominent—created opportunities for many players who had the training camps to themselves. The strike began on July 1 and ended on August 10. Preseason games were manned mostly by rookies, and the Steelers finished the preseason with a 3–0 record.

It should be noted that when the vets finally joined practices, they knew they had a lot of work to do. The frontline players felt secure, but the backups knew they were up against talented rookies who already had weeks of practice and preseason games under their belts. Rocky Bleier, who had not yet established himself, remembers just trying to make the team; he was more focused on his own battle to survive and did not yet realize the potential of that rookie group. John Stallworth was pleased that there was very little rookie hazing since the veteran players were too committed to preparing for the fast-approaching season.

Some 1974 Steeler veteran players are quick to remind people that although the 1974 rookie class paved the way for the impending dynasty of the Steelers, Jack Lambert was the only full-time starter. However, as the season progressed, Swann and Stallworth gradually supplanted starters Ron Shanklin and Frank Lewis, and by playoff time, they were getting far more playing time than the veterans.

THE HALL OF FAMERS

First Round: Lynn Swann, University of Southern California

Art Rooney Jr., the Steeler personnel VP, remembers USC head coach John McKay telling him that Swann was the greatest competitor he had ever coached and that Swann's uncanny jumping ability and great hands would make him a great NFL player. Lynn Swann's injuries limited his initial practice sessions in his 1974 rookie training camp, but John Stallworth noted early on that even though Swann had not yet made an impression with his skills, he admired Lynn's extreme confidence and poise, noting how comfortable he was with the coaches and the media. A Blesto scouting combine scout from the west area, Howard White, had obtained a 4.55 grass time before the draft, which confirmed that Swann would have the necessary speed to be a front-line NFL wide receiver and would help overcome his 5'11", 180-pound size. But Swann's production as a big-time Pac-10 player was a definite asset.

Swann and Stallworth would both have relatively quiet rookie seasons until the playoffs as the Steelers went on to win their first Super Bowl with a 16–6 victory over the Minnesota Vikings in New Orleans. Swann and Stallworth enjoyed much more playing time than the starters Ron Shanklin and Frank Lewis during the playoffs.

Swann's regular season statistics were 11 receptions for 208 yards and 2 touchdowns, but he did lead the NFL in punt returns, and the production in that area was the fourth best in NFL history at that time. He enjoyed a breakout season in 1975 and went on to a career that showed four Super Bowl victories with an MVP in Super Bowl X for the winning touchdown, making a catch that is still a Super Bowl highlight. He played in three Pro Bowls and was named All-Pro in 1975, 1977 and 1978. He retired after the 1982 season and was inducted into the NFL Hall of Fame in 2001.

Second Round: Jack Lambert, Kent State

Lambert was a one-year college middle backer after playing defensive end as an underclassman. Rocky Bleier remembers "the tall, skinny guy who kept showing up in the Steelers offices after the draft." Lambert impressed Steeler coaches when he drove to Pittsburgh from Kent State in Ohio while he was still in college to begin studying under linebacker coach Woody Widenhofer. He was originally lined up on the depth chart behind outside linebacker Jack Ham, but training camp injuries to veteran middle linebackers Henry Davis and Ed Bradley allowed him to be moved inside. Davis had started all games in 1972 and 1973 and had made the 1973 Pro Bowl roster. Lambert became the only member of the 1974 rookie class who was a full-time starter. He went to nine consecutive Pro Bowls and four Super Bowls; won honors as the NFL Defensive Rookie of the Year and NFL Defensive Player of the Year in 1976; and was a member of the NFL Anniversary All-Time team. He retired in 1984 and was inducted into the NFL Hall of Fame in 1990.

Fourth Round: John Stallworth Alabama A&M

Stallworth remembers that his rookie teammates were very cocky because they had the run of the training camp before the veterans made their late arrival because of the veteran players' training camp strike. He also recalls that once the veterans arrived there, was very little hazing by the vets, who just wanted to get to work once they arrived. His position coach, Lionel Taylor, said Stallworth was making a strong impression. He warned John that things would change once the veterans arrived, especially another future Hall of Famer, Mel Blount. Stallworth loved Taylor; he knew that he needed him to achieve the development he required to become a solid NFL receiver.

Lionel taught Stallworth how to prepare and practice, and Stallworth remembers how tough he was on him. Stallworth once grew angry with Taylor because he thought he was unfairly singled out for criticism, but Taylor told him he was so much better than the other players that Taylor's expectations were much higher. But Stallworth also remembers that Taylor took him to his home to meet his family and did all he could to help him.

Stallworth started three games in his rookie 1974 season with modest production but had increased playing time during that season's playoff. He went on to set Super Bowl records with a 24.4 average for catch, and in Super Bowl XIV, he averaged 40.3 per catch. He played 14 seasons and played in four Super Bowls. He retired after the 1987 season and was inducted into the NFL Hall of Fame in 2002.

John founded Madison Research Corporation in 1986 and on March 23, 2009, became a minority owner of the Pittsburgh Steelers.

Fifth Round: Mike Webster, Wisconsin

Webster, aptly, was born in Tomahawk, Wisconsin. He weighed 235 at the East/West Shrine Bowl and his 6'1" stature was far below what most NFL teams wanted, but he suited the Steeler mold for undersized, athletic, tough and smart linemen. John Stallworth remembers being surprised at how small he was, but Webster very early showed how extraordinary he was, especially in his training camp battles against Jack Lambert. He became a full-time starter in 1975, played in 245 games with 217 starts, went to nine Pro Bowls and was elected to the NFL Hall of Fame in 1997. He retired in March 1991 after playing two seasons with the Kansas City Chiefs.

Free Agent: Donnie Shell, South Carolina State University

Shell was a linebacker at South Carolina State University, and he was doing his practice teaching requirement when Bill Nunn called him after the draft. Houston and Denver were also interested, but his coach, Willie Jeffries, convinced him Pittsburgh would be the best option for him and Nunn signed him for a $1,000 bonus. Nunn had convinced Art Rooney Jr. that Shell had the tools for NFL secondary play.

Once he arrived in training camp, he and John Stallworth bonded, since they had played against each other in college and shared the same background. Shell remembers that the 1974 rookie group in training camp was a very competitive one that practiced at a very high-intensity level. He recalls that when the veterans arrived, they treated the rookies with respect and admired how the rookies did not back down when challenged.

Players remember that Shell hit veteran receiver Jon Staggers in practice with such force that Staggers was staggering around, dazed, after the hit. Shell was worried that coach Chuck Noll would be angry, but Noll smiled and immediately praised him. That incident earned him the nickname "Torpedo" from veteran Dwight White, who coined most of the nicknames for his teammates. His hit on Earl Campbell during a December 1978 victory against the Houston Oilers showed the football world why he was the Torpedo.

Shell started one game in 1974, became a full-time 1977 starter and started 11 consecutive seasons. He played in five Pro Bowls between 1978 and 1982, and he was three-time First Team All-Pro. He finished his career with 51 interceptions and had at least one interception each year of his career. He retired in 1987 and was inducted into the NFL Hall of Fame in 2020.

CHAPTER 18

1974: AMOEBA DOMINANCE

PITT BASKETBALL HITS THE ELITE EIGHT

By David Finoli

I   t's the details in sports that sometimes get lost. Pitt fans know that the 1973–74 basketball team had a memorable season. While they remember the efforts of All-American Billy Knight, they may not recall that the Panthers' success was set up by a remarkable defense their coach Buzz Ridl instituted called the Amoeba Defense.

According to the website Microscope Clarity, the word *amoeba* derives "from the Greek word *amoibe* which means 'to change.' These microscopic organisms are often called 'shape-shifters' as they have the ability to constantly change their shape." Taking it to basketball terms, it's a defense that mixes both man-to-man and zone defense. When the Amoeba Defense is working properly, the offense has no idea what it's facing, and it can be very disruptive. The players are set up in a diamond with the quick guards out front, a big center below under the basket and the two forwards on each side of the lane. While it's high risk and can be ineffective if not done properly, the Pitt Panthers of 1973–74 played it almost to perfection.

While Ridl is often given credit for the defense—as at times was his assistant and successor Tim Grgurich, who took it with him to UNLV, where it was utilized successfully by Jerry Tarkanian during the Running Rebels championship run—it was actually developed by Ridl's other assistant Fran Webster, who wrote a book on the subject titled *Basketball's Amoeba Defense*. Kirk Bruce, a guard on the team, stated in an article in the *Pittsburgh Post-Gazette*, "There were so many times when we felt like we really had the other

Pitt basketball coach Buzz Ridl, who led the program to a memorable Elite Eight run in the 1974 NCAA Tournament. He did it by running the Amoeba Defense and recruiting the best talent Western Pennsylvania had to offer at a time when most local high school elite players left the area to continue their collegiate careers. *Photo courtesy of the University of Pittsburgh Athletics.*

team baffled, and there were other times when we were equally confused, but it usually worked itself out because we were pretty aggressive."

The other unique thing about this ball club was that it was made up of mostly local players at a time when high school basketball in Western Pennsylvania wasn't exactly among the best in the nation and most players who were of Division I quality usually left the city to continue their collegiate careers. All five starters and the top sub were from the area. An article by Rick Shrum in the *Pittsburgh Post-Gazette* celebrating the team's 25th anniversary pointed out that "*Sports Illustrated* ran a photo of the starters and first sub grouped on an observation deck atop Mount Washington, and the perception that all six could see their homes from there wasn't far from correct."

Bruce went to South Hills High School, while Knight was a product of Braddock, center Jim Bolla was from Central Catholic, forward Mickey Martin was a Baldwin man, sixth man Keith Starr came from Quaker

Valley and guard Tom Richards was a Moon High School grad. Grgurich was the main recruiter who successfully kept this talent in the area, but make no mistake, it was Ridl who pushed it to heights the team hadn't seen since 1941.

Hired from Westminster College in 1968, where he won an NAIA National Championship, Ridl took over for Bob Timmons, who was let go after four consecutive poor seasons. Buzz did no better his first year as the 1968–69 Panthers finished with a 4–20 mark. The next year, the team improved to 12–12 but languished around the .500 for two seasons following a 14–10 record in 1970–71. The Panthers were only 12–14 in 1972–73, but Ridl felt they were not far away, losing several close games. In his mind, they just needed to learn how to close games. In a *Pittsburgh Press* article before a season opening game against West Virginia in Morgantown, he said, "We couldn't handle close games last year. We could have had eight more wins. We're hoping the year of experience will help." Following a close loss to the Mountaineers 82–78 in the opener, it seemed like they hadn't learned. Was it going to be another frustrating season? After an 82–65 rout of crosstown rival Duquesne at the Civic Arena, Pitt proved to be a quick learner. From December 7 through February 20, they did not lose a game, going on a memorable 22-game winning streak.

Winning the first 14 of the streak by double digit margins until their 68–62 victory at William & Mary, Pitt took on their toughest opponents of the season, Syracuse, on February 9, with the streak at 18. Ranked 10th at the time in the Associated Press poll, Pitt was greeted by a capacity crowd of 5,308 at the Fitzgerald Field House, and the atmosphere was electric. Knight had come into the game with a badly bruised shoulder, and their number two scorer, Martin, had nerve damage in his leg. Despite these injuries, they both were on the court at game time, where Knight—who averaged 21.8 points per game as well as 13.4 rebounds and was named a first team All-American at the end of the season on the United States Basketball Writers Association squad—had 21 points and 19 rebounds in a surprisingly one-sided 71–56 victory. The win vaulted them into the top 10 in the AP poll for the first time, landing them at number seven.

Pitt eventually stretched the streak to 22 before late-season losses to Penn State and 14th-ranked South Carolina. They ended the regular season with a revenge victory over WVU to finish the season 22–3, which helped them land a spot in the NCAA tourney. They defeated St Joseph's 54–42 in the first round before a close 81–78 victory in the Sweet Sixteen against Furman as Knight was at his best with 34 points. It propelled the Panthers to the

Elite Eight, the furthest the team had advanced in the tourney in 33 years. Their prize was a contest against top-ranked North Carolina State and their legend David Thompson.

There had been rumors before the season that this might be Ridl's final season if the team didn't improve (he would actually only coach one more year at Pitt). But chancellor Wesley Posvar made it clear that Buzz could coach at the school as long as he wanted to.

In the quarterfinal, Pitt had kept it close early on and was hopeful it could pull off the upset after Thompson went up for an aggressive slam dunk, ended up landing on his head and was lost for the game. What hope the team had of pulling off the upset and landing in the Final Four ended quickly when the Wolf Pack's 7–4 center Rick Burleson led NC State to a dominant 100–72 win.

Disappointing ending aside, the team finished 25–4, having what is still arguably its greatest season in the modern era of Pitt basketball. Richards said it best when he exclaimed, "It was just a wonderful experience. It was a great lesson of people understanding what their roll is in the success of a whole unit." It also didn't hurt that the team had a thorough understanding of the Amoeba Defense, either.

CHAPTER 19

1974: KINGS OF THE EAST ONCE AGAIN

By Frank Garland

There was no telling what to expect from the 1974 Pittsburgh Pirates. Coming off a season in which they struggled to replace their departed superstar Roberto Clemente, the Bucs were dealt a double whammy in 1973 when starting pitcher Steve Blass, one of the best in the National League the previous year, inexplicably lost the ability to throw a strike.

Somehow, the '73 Pirates persevered, though, and after scuffling midway through the season, rallied to take over first place in the National League East midway through September after a managerial switch that saw second-year skipper Bill Virdon replaced by old reliable Danny Murtaugh.

The Pirates managed to hold on to the lead for nine days before falling off the pace and eventually finishing in third place, three games behind the eventual World Champion New York Mets.

The '73 club wound up with a lackluster 80–82 mark—the first time since 1968 the team finished below .500. Still, some prognosticators expected good things for '74, and in fact, Bob Smizik of the *Pittsburgh Press* picked the Bucs to easily win the NL East thanks to the division's best hitting lineup and a solid starting pitching rotation.

But things didn't go according to plan, at least for the first half of the season and beyond. On June 7, the Pirates found themselves 14 games under .500 and mired in last place in the division. Players were already griping; in April, Al Oliver complained about being moved from center field to first base. Later, erstwhile starter Dock Ellis balked at Murtaugh's decision to move him to the bullpen.

Ellis declared, "There is no way I'll relieve with this club…not for one game, not for one inning, not for one pitch," *Post-Gazette* beat writer Charley Feeney reported.

Murtaugh, never one to get excited, responded, "Dock will relieve if I tell him to."

Ellis's outburst came on the heels of outfielder Richie Zisk blasting Murtaugh after the veteran leader moved the young outfielder into a platoon role with Dave Parker—a move Zisk learned about from a reporter.

"Someone is being lied to here," Zisk told Smizik. "Murtaugh has got to realize he's not dealing with seven-year-olds. Him and his Irish philosophy.

"You know that no one is blaming Murtaugh for our struggles now, so I hope when we straighten things out no one will be patting him on the back. I think this is a good indication that Bill Virdon's firing was unjustified."

As if things were not going badly enough, the team lost a key arm when right-hander Bob Moose underwent emergency surgery in late May to remove a blood clot that had developed between his clavicle and his first rib—an operation that would sideline him for the rest of the season.

Despite all the trials and tribulations, the Pirates somehow managed to regain their footing and stormed back into the NL East race. From their low-water mark of 18–32 on June 7, the club went 70–42 (a .625 clip) and a double-header sweep of the San Diego Padres on August 25 enabled them to vault into first place, a position that they retained at least a share of the rest of the way.

Many players were responsible for that surge. Slugger Willie Stargell batted .318 with 19 homers and 67 RBIs during the final 93 games of his season, checking in with an OPS of 1.011 during that stretch. Al Oliver, the steady line-drive machine, hit at a .342 clip with an .875 OPS from June 10 through the end of the season, driving in 63 runs. The aforementioned Zisk, who ended up appearing in 149 games and coming to the plate 604 times, batted .313 with 17 home runs and 100 RBIs, 72 of which came in his final 104 games.

On the mound, four of the five primary starters won at least 12 games— Jerry Reuss (16), Jim Rooker (15), Ken Brett (13) and Ellis (12). Veteran reliever Dave Giusti appeared in 64 and finished 41 of them, collecting 12 saves, and Ramón Hernández worked in 58 games, compiling a 2.75 ERA. Blass, meanwhile, appeared in just one game, giving up five hits and eight runs—five of them earned—in five innings of work.

While many of the Bucs put together outstanding individual seasons, the NL East title did not come easy. The Pirates never led by more than two games, and as the calendar turned from September to October, the club was tied for first with the St. Louis Cardinals with just two games to play.

It took a dramatic two-run pinch-hit home run by Bob Robertson in the eighth inning of the next-to-last game for the Pirates to beat the Chicago Cubs, 6–5, and clinch a tie for first on a cold, rainy night at Three Rivers Stadium, thanks to the Montreal Expos' 3–2 win over the Cards.

Robertson, prone to the strikeout, had no trouble explaining what happened. "I got my pitch and I hit it good," said the muscular first baseman known to many Pirates fans as "the Maryland Strongboy," thanks to Pirates announcer Bob Prince. "That's baseball. I could have popped it up. That's usually the kind of pitch I foul back or miss."

That set the stage for the regular-season finale—and more late heroics. On the regular season's final day, the Bucs clinched their fourth NL East title in five years by pulling out yet another one-run win, this time by a 5–4 count over the Cubs. This one was even more improbable than the previous day's victory.

Pittsburgh spotted the visitors a 4–0 lead and trailed 4–2 entering the bottom of the ninth but cut the deficit to one on Parker's fielder's choice. That brought Robertson up to pinch hit against Rick Reuschel, with Manny Sanguillen stationed at third base with the potential tying run and two outs. Reuschel had a full count on Robertson, then uncorked a sharp slider that Robertson swung and missed for strike three. But Cubs catcher Steve Swisher could not corral the pitch, then uncorked a throw to first that hit Robertson in the shoulder and bounced behind first base. That allowed Sanguillen to score from third, tying the game at 4–4.

The Pirates won it in the 10th on Oliver's one-out triple, a pair of intentional walks and Sanguillen's topped roller to third base, which charging Cubs third baseman Bill Madlock tried to barehand but could not come up with, allowing Oliver to score the division-clinching run.

A return to the World Series was not to be for the '74 Bucs, as they ran into a Los Angeles Dodgers team that won a Major League–best 102 games during the regular season—14 more than the Pirates. The Dodgers took the first two games, 3–0 and 5–2, at Three Rivers, leaving Pittsburgh no margin for error. The Pirates gave their fans a glimmer of hope by blanking Los Angeles 7–0 in Game 3, but that hope was snuffed out in Game 4 when the Dodgers romped to a 12–1 victory, securing the NL pennant. Unlike the heart-wrenching Game 5 loss to the Reds two years earlier, this one wasn't so tough to take, and it didn't dent the psyche of that Pirate team.

"Our attitude was the same, every day and every year," Oliver said in a 2022 interview, referring to the Pirates of the 1970s, who won five division titles during his nine-year stay in Pittsburgh. "We always thought we were better than the team we were playing. The Pittsburgh Pirates never lacked confidence at all."

CHAPTER 20

1974: THE TRUE BEGINNING OF A DYNASTY

THE STEELERS WIN SUPER BOWL IX

By David Finoli

It's said by many that the Steeler dynasty began when rookie running back Franco Harris snatched a deflected pass off the chest of Oakland Raider defensive back Jack Tatum (yes, I know the argument is that the ball hit Pittsburgh running back Frenchy Fuqua, but from what I see, there is no way the ball pops that far back unless Tatum hit it—and yes, I'm a devout Steeler fan, but still) and made what appeared to be a useless fourth down incompletion into the famed Immaculate Reception. While the play was dramatic, the team wasn't a championship franchise at that point. To me, it was the draft of 1974 and a defensive effort in the postseason that year that took this team to another level. It was at this point the dynasty truly began.

It wasn't that the previous two seasons weren't special. Up until 1972, the franchise had pretty much been the laughingstock of the National Football League. It had been in exactly one playoff game, a forgettable 21–0 loss to the cross-state Philadelphia Eagles when the two were tied at the top of the Eastern Division standings in 1947. They had won exactly zero division titles and more often than not were challenging for the number one pick in the college draft.

That all seemed to end with a Central Division crown in '72, their first postseason win against the Raiders and a return to the playoffs a year later. As good as they had done, it still looked like there was some work to do

Chuck Noll (No. 41), pictured with his hand on the Governor's Cup while playing at the University of Dayton, eventually became one of the greatest coaches ever to man the sidelines in the NFL. He became the first coach to lead four teams to Super Bowl championships in league history. *Photo courtesy of the University of Dayton Athletics.*

to make the next step and compete for a Super Bowl championship. Now that they were a successful team, elite positions in the draft were becoming something of the past as they would pick 21st out of the 26 NFL teams. Not really a prime spot to have the greatest draft a North American major professional sports team would enjoy, but luckily for the Steelers and their staff, that's what was about to happen.

Tim Rooney goes into this in a much more in-depth manner in chapter 17, but to give a quick summation, Pittsburgh took Lynn Swann out of USC with the first pick. In round two, they selected un undersized 6'4½", 215-pound middle linebacker (quarterback Terry Bradshaw also weighed 215 pounds, for comparison) with a nasty demeanor by the name of Jack Lambert. There was no third-round pick, but they had two in the fourth, the first being a *Pittsburgh Courier* All-American receiver out of Alabama A&M named John Stallworth, and the second being the answer to the trivia question "Which one of the first five Steeler picks did not make the Hall of Fame?" The answer: Jimmy Allen, a defensive back from UCLA. In round five, they took the heir apparent to center Ray Mansfield, who hailed from Wisconsin: Mike Webster. Add to the mix an undrafted rookie free agent safety from South Carolina State who went by the name of Donnie Shell, and the rookie crop of 1974 gave the Steelers five future Pro Football Hall of Famers to add to their already impressive roster.

As the season was beginning, the league was experiencing their first work stoppage, which gave the rookies extra practice time at preseason camp in Latrobe to catch the eye of coach Chuck Noll. It also gave those veterans who crossed the picket line, like quarterback Joe Gilliam, some time to show the coaches exactly how talented they were. In 1974, players often had to work second jobs to make ends meet, as the minimum salary was only $12,500 and many who had a few years' experience were making between $20,000 and $40,000. Raider great Phil Villapiano recalled in a Pro Football Research Association (PFRA) article in their magazine *Coffin Corner*, "We didn't get paid for the pre-season. For six games you had to get your ass kicked for no money. And they gave us $17 a day per diem, but is that right? You know it was so wrong, but we put up with it because we loved football." The Steelers, through their six games, went undefeated in the preseason. Gilliam was proving to be the superior quarterback. The union was not strong, and certainly the veterans like Bradshaw were afraid of losing their jobs, so little by little, they were crossing the line to get back into camp.

Bradshaw denied coming back because he was afraid of losing his job, stating in a *Pittsburgh Post-Gazette* article that "I considered showing up three weeks ago and again last Tuesday, but I was told to wait a spell, that things in the strike were going to happen. A quarterback, you know, is in a position where so much is involved. I stayed out for 'the cause' and out of respect for my teammates but the big issue now is right here with me. I'm 25 years old and I had a decision to make and I have to stick by it." Unfortunately for the former number one pick in the draft, Gilliam kept impressing the coaches and, by opening day against the Baltimore Colts, became the starting quarterback.

Gilliam was impressive in his first two contests, a 30–0 win against the Colts, where he hit Swann with a perfect 54-yard touchdown bomb, and then tossing for 348 yards at Denver in a 35–35 tie, but his production began to diminish, and Chuck Noll became uncomfortable with Gilliam's "pass first" philosophy (quarterbacks called the plays back then). Despite the fact the team stood at 4–1–1, Bradshaw was eventually given his starting spot

Joe Greene (No. 75) is widely considered the greatest player ever to don a Pittsburgh Steeler uniform. In 1974, he briefly considered quitting when he thought the team wasn't close to being a championship contender. By the season's end, those thoughts vanished as the team captured its first NFL title. *Photo courtesy of North Texas State University Athletics.*

back after a miserable 5 for 18 performance by Gilliam against the Cleveland Browns and kept it through the rest of the season.

The team played well through most of the season, but following a 13–10 loss to Houston, they stood only 8–3–1 and looked as if they had made no progress over the past two years. This frustrated their all-world defensive tackle Joe Greene, who hated to lose with a passion and decided he had enough and temporarily quit the team. In a CBS Sports online article, the Steeler great said, "I went to my locker and picked up my belongings and got into my car. My thoughts were that…I don't know what they were, but I was leaving because I was disappointed. But in the midst of all of that, I said, 'Boy, I sure hope that somebody comes out here and stops me.'" That person who stopped him turned out to be wide receivers coach Lionel Taylor. "He sat down in the car and we talked. I don't know what we talked about, but anyway, I was glad we talked, because I went back. And that's when it started."

Pittsburgh won their final two games to capture the central again and then dominated the Buffalo Bills 32–14 in the first round of the playoffs, holding Hall of Fame running back O.J. Simpson to only 49 yards in the process. It was the beginning of what would be a dominating postseason by the legendary Steel Curtain defense.

Traveling to Oakland the next week for the AFC Championship, where the Raiders crushed them in a 1973 postseason matchup 33–14, Pittsburgh frustrated Raider runners, holding Oakland to 29 yards on 21 attempts in the process, yet trailed 10–7 going into the final quarter. At that point, Franco Harris and Rocky Bleier took over as they ran for 111 and 98 yards respectively, leading Pittsburgh to 21 fourth-quarter points and a 24–13 win that put the franchise in their first NFL championship game, against the Minnesota Vikings in Super Bowl IX.

The offensive game plan that day at Tulane Stadium (the game was supposed to be played at the palatial new Super Dome, but it wasn't completed at that point) was to give the ball to Franco Harris. Regardless of the venue, the game's MVP rambled for what was then a Super Bowl record: 158 yards. With the defense playing at an amazing level, the game was much more one-sided than the 16–6 final score might have suggested. Minnesota ran for only 17 yards on 20 carries and had a mere 123 yards of total offense. Pittsburgh scored only a safety by Dwight White in the first half, but a nine-yard touchdown run by Harris in the third and a four-yard touchdown pass from Bradshaw to then tight end Larry Brown overshadowed the Vikings' lone score on a blocked Bobby Walden punt to give owner Art Rooney and his franchise their first league championship in a 16–6 victory.

While it didn't have the flair of the Immaculate Reception, this nonetheless was the day the Steeler dynasty truly began.

CHAPTER 21

1975: KISS HIM GOODBYE

THE PIRATES FIRE LEGENDARY BROADCASTER
BOB PRINCE

By David Finoli

For decades, Pittsburgh Pirate fans were given the news of the team's exploits by one of the greatest broadcasters ever to sit behind the mike. His name was Bob "the Gunner" Prince, and his colorful sayings and anecdotes were part of a Pirate fans language as they stayed glued to their radios. That all ended following the 1975 campaign when the legendary broadcaster was given his walking papers in a move that stunned the Pirate nation.

After beginning his broadcasting career with a radio show on WJAS-AM in Pittsburgh, Prince was given a shot in the Pirate booth with the equally legendary Pirate announcer Rosey Rowswell in 1947 after Jack Craddock resigned. They were both similar in how they approached the game, with colorful stories in more of an entertaining mode rather than a straight play-by-play approach. Rowswell thought Prince might be trying to upstage him and limited his partner's time on the air. As Prince confided in his Society of American Baseball Research (SABR) bio online, "I had to convince Rosey that I wasn't out to upstage him. When he learned I was sincere we worked well together."

Sadly, Rowswell died in February 1955, and Prince took over his duties as the main play-by-play man in the Pirate booth. He was an unabashed homer, which came out when he was helping to broadcast the 1971 World Series for NBC as the Bucs took on the Baltimore Orioles. That was OK, because that's just how Prince was. He brought several unique sayings into the booth, such as "Kiss it goodbye," "Arriba" (when hoping Clemente would hit a homer), "The bases are FOB" (full of Bucs), "A bloop and a blast," "Chicken on the hill with Will" (promising to give chicken away at Willie Stargell's restaurant when he'd hit a home run), "Hidden vigorish," "How sweet it is" and " We had 'em all the way," just to name a few.

Prince was also very close to the players, even arranging a plane to take hurler Bruce Kison to his wedding following the Pirates' seventh game victory in Baltimore at the '71 Series. He would give them unique nicknames, such as Dave "the Cobra" Parker, Vern "the Deacon" Law, Bob "Doggie" Skinner, Gene "Little Angry" Clines, Harvey "the Kitten" Haddix and Don "the Tiger" Hoak. His style was embraced by many Pirate fans but was also irritating to many others, including some sponsors and some members of the front office.

General manager Branch Rickey was more a fan of a straight play-by-play approach and thought Prince's style was off base. His successor Joe L. Brown would complain that the Hall of Fame announcer needed to sell the team more and frequently gave him notes about what he needed to do, often monitoring his broadcasts. He thought as Prince went on, he often would stray too far away from the action. KDKA-AM radio owner Westinghouse Broadcasting, which owned the rights to broadcast Pirate games, agreed. The company allowed guests into the spacious broadcasting booth at Three Rivers Stadium, which upset the Gunner, causing him a few times to complain about it on the air. The team began to sell the seats in the back of the booth, which further enraged Prince. In a *Pittsburgh Post-Gazette* article, he said, "It has never happened anywhere in the history of baseball. I consider the booth my office. I don't know who is responsible for selling the tickets but it isn't right."

The relationship between Westinghouse and Prince, as well as between Brown and his broadcaster, became strained as the mid-'70s approached. Prince did become indignant toward his bosses, most likely thinking he was untouchable, and his ramblings on air about subjects other than baseball became more commonplace. Little by little, as the 1975 season was coming to a close, persistent rumors swirled that Prince was unhappy and might entertain other offers and that his broadcast partner, former Pirate pitcher Nellie King, was not going to have his contract renewed. Prince confided in August that year that his disputes with Westinghouse almost led him to take the job as top man for the San Diego Padres in 1969, but he felt the Padres weren't going to spend money to field a contender, so he stayed with Pittsburgh.

After the 1975 season concluded, it was reported in late October that King's contract would, in fact, not be renewed and that the Gunner's job was not secure. Later that day, on October 30, the shocking news was confirmed: both King and Prince would not be back in 1976, and a new tandem would be selected to replace them. King claimed that "they say it was a joint agreement." The club owners, the rights owners and KDKA got together and voted. The town was in an uproar. These men that the Pirate faithful considered family were now gone. Iron City Beer, the main sponsor, came out and claimed it had voted to keep the two and didn't want them fired but that it only had one-third of the vote and lost out. It didn't matter to the many who decided to quit drinking Iron City in protest because they were a part of the unsavory situation. Westinghouse vice president Edward Wallis, who was not a Prince fan, disputed Iron City's claim, saying, "The decision was unanimous."

The news came around election day, and politicians came out in support of the Bucs broadcasters. Commissioner William Hunt said, "The love affair between the Pittsburgh Pirates and all of Western Pennsylvania was nurtured by these two personable voices and you have destroyed that love affair." A protest parade was quickly planned, and 10,000 people turned out to support their fallen heroes. To the dismay of Pirate management, several players showed up to support the broadcasters, including Stargell, Kison, Dave Giusti, Al Oliver and Jim Rooker.

It was for naught, as King eventually hooked on as sports information director and announcer at Duquesne University for basketball, and a depressed Prince, who reportedly didn't leave his bedroom for three days following the dismissal, went from one job to another with the Astros and on Monday Night Baseball for ABC as well as an ill-fated shift as an announcer for the Pittsburgh Penguins. All were met with failure, as Prince was lost until being brought back into the Pirate booth again, first in the early '80s on a new cable network in the area and then finally back to his old job on KDKA in 1985, where he came back to an emotional Three Rivers Stadium on May 3. Unfortunately, his comeback was very limited. He had cancer and was admitted to the hospital shortly after, where he died on June 10.

Prince was a part of the community, worked hard for charities and was a confidant for many players during his time with the Bucs. His replacement, Milo Hamilton, would never have the chance to be embraced, as Pirate fans looked at him with disdain through no fault of his own, although he would blame Prince for making his life in Pittsburgh difficult through his lack of support. It was an impossible gig, as their hero Prince was gone, a sad moment in Pirate history when the team and its broadcast partner "kissed him goodbye."

CHAPTER 22

1975: THE RYDER CUP
COMES TO LAUREL VALLEY

By David Finoli

Once upon a time, the Ryder Cup wasn't exactly an intense competition where evenly matched teams went after each other aggressively and the outcome usually went down to the last match of the final day. The teams didn't wear uniforms and celebrate with champagne baths following an emotional victory. When the Ryder Cup came to one of Arnold Palmer's favorite venues in 1975, the Laurel Valley Country Club in Ligonier, it was generally a one-sided affair where the best the United States had to offer easily thrashed the top golfers in England and Ireland. Oh yeah—and there weren't tens of thousands of fans crammed into every nook and cranny of the course. Of course, today the event doesn't have to go up against a Pittsburgh Pirate/St. Louis Cardinal series with the Bucs approaching an Eastern Division championship, nor does it have to fight to take away the attention of the Steeler nation, which was rooting for a defending Super Bowl champion.

Laurel Valley in the latter part of the 20th century was a favorite venue of the PGA tour. Designed by Dick Wilson and Arnold Palmer in 1959, it has hosted the 1965 PGA Championship, the 1989 U.S. Senior Open, the Marconi Classic in 2001 and the 2005 Senior PGA Championship, among several other PGA Tour events. The impressive par 71, 7,154-yard course, which is rated as the fifth best in Pennsylvania according to *Golf Digest*, was generally chosen to host events to honor its most famous member, Palmer, who was the U.S. captain for the Cup in 1975. If it hosted the Cup

A statue of Latrobe's most famous son, Arnold Palmer, which stands at the airport that bears his name. Palmer is the unquestioned greatest golfer Western Pennsylvania ever produced, although he never was able to win a major at Oakmont during his Hall of Fame career. *Photo courtesy of David Finoli.*

in today's world, it wouldn't have to aggressively advertise tickets—they would be snapped up moments after they went on sale—but in the week leading up to the event, there were many ads in the paper, hoping area golf fans would be interested in attending the event in this majestic part of Western Pennsylvania.

On the Monday prior to the Ryder Cup, sportswriter Ray Kienzel scripted a column in the *Pittsburgh Press* where he wondered if the club would draw 5,000 people to each day of the event. He pointed out what the Cup was up against. The Pirates' magic number to clinch the division was two, as they were hosting the Cards; the Steelers were beginning the defense of their Super Bowl crown in San Diego at four o'clock on Sunday as the Ryder Cup would be possibly coming down to its most important matches. That weekend, Penn State would be playing Ohio State; and hell, even the annual Latrobe Air Show was going on, and Palmer desperately wanted to see the precision flying. Ed Carter, who was in charge of promoting the event, disputed Kienzel's claim, but not by much: "I think we'll do more than 5,000. But I think 8,000 to 10,000 is as good as we can expect."

It wasn't as if there was much drama in the Ryder Cups of that era. Except for a 16–16 tie in 1969 when Jack Nicklaus famously conceded a shot to Tony Jacklin—which wasn't exactly an easy shot—to give Great Britain the tie, England hadn't won the cup since 1957 and had only captured three the first 20 times the event was played. To make matters worse, according to *Pittsburgh Press* sports editor Pat Livingston, this was the best U.S. team ever created. And he wasn't wrong. The 46-year-old Palmer was a nonplaying captain, and he had the following golfers at his disposal: Billy Casper, Ray Floyd, Al Geiberger, Lou Graham, Hale Irwin, Gene Littler, Johnny Miller, Bob Murphy, J.C. Snead, Lee Trevino, Tom Weiskopf and arguably the greatest ever to swing a golf club in Nicklaus. These were golfers who had won 22 PGA events and $1.9 million in 1975 winnings, a huge amount at the time. When compared to who British captain Bernard Hunt was putting up—namely Brian Barnes, Maurice Bembridge, Eamonn Darcy, Bernard Gallacher, Tommy Horton, Brian Hugett, Guy Hunt, Christy O'Connor Jr., John O'Leary, Peter Oosterhuis, Norman Wood and Jacklin—a mismatch was definitely a possibility. It was a who's who of Hall of Fame golfers versus a collection of "Who is that?"

Despite the fact that a rout was on the horizon, Palmer put things into perspective in a *Pittsburgh Press* article. "If (Peter) Oosterhuis beats somebody like (Jack) Nicklaus or (Lee) Trevino, that's a big victory for the British team. If they win only five matches all week, each will be a big personal victory."

He went on to say that "the players are giving up their time to play for their country and if they lose, they will have lost more than a golf match; they will have lost a great deal of honor." Talk about putting pressure on these guys.

As the United States took on their opponents in the four alternate shot matches in the morning on a soggy golf course following a heavy rain the previous day, it was apparent the rout that everyone expected was about to take place. About 4,000 patrons were on the muddy course that morning, and they witnessed the United States sweeping all four matches. So dominant were they that the Brits only led any of the matches at one particular time, when O'Leary dropped a 25-foot putt at the 11th to put his team up temporarily by one hole. Nicklaus and Weiskopf crushed Barnes and Gallacher 5-and-4, while Irwin and Littler took theirs 5 and 3 with magnificent play at the 13th, 14th and 15th. The rout was now on.

In the afternoon four-ball matches, Britain and Ireland did get on the board as Oosterhuis and Jacklin defeated Casper and Floyd 2 and 1, and Barnes and Gallacher halved their match with Nicklaus and Murphy. Weiskopf and Graham and Trevino and Murphy each won their matches as the United States ended the first day with a 6½ to 1½ lead.

The next day, Huggett, who hadn't played the first day, teamed with Jacklin to beat Trevino and Murphy in the afternoon alternate shot matches. Unfortunately, it turned out to be England's only victory in the four afternoon matches. That was coupled with only one point in the morning better ball matches as Darcy and Hunt split their match with Geiberger and Floyd after Darcy made a clutch birdie on 18 and Oosterhuis and Jacklin blew a lead against Miller and Casper to tie their match. While there was controversy regarding Huggett not playing on the first day, as many players thought the rules should be changed so everyone could play on all days, the main talk was how superior the U.S. team was with a now almost insurmountable 12½ to 3½ lead.

There would be 16 singles matches on the final day, with the United States needing to win just four to clinch taking the Ryder Cup once again. While the Brits played better in the eight morning matches, the United States got the points they needed when Casper defeated Darby 3 and 2 to clinch a tie and Weiskopf beat Hunt 5 and 3 to give them the victory. There was a huge upset in the morning when Barnes beat Nicklaus 4 and 2.

With a win in hand, Palmer wanted the Bear to get his revenge, so he made sure he'd be paired with Barnes in the afternoon. Palmer told the *Pittsburgh Press* that "the Barnes-Nicklaus pairing was not by chance. I went and got the British pairings and found where Barnes was and put Nicklaus there on my lineup....When I saw he (Nicklaus) got beat this morning, I thought he deserved another chance." Even though the captain's heart was in the right place, Nicklaus was once again upset by Barnes in the afternoon. This time it was 2 and 1.

With the United States up $17\frac{1}{2}$ to $6\frac{1}{2}$ going into the afternoon matches, the 7,000 fans who showed up on another rainy day saw Britain's best finally do well. With the match out of hand, they won the afternoon matches $4\frac{1}{2}$ to $3\frac{1}{2}$, although it wasn't enough to avoid humiliation in a 21 to 11 loss.

With the luster going out of the event with the United States so dominant, following another British loss in 1977, the format changed from the United States versus Great Britain and Ireland to the USA going up against the best Europe had to offer. It evened up the teams and made for the dramatic popular event that the Ryder Cup has become. In 1975, though, it was a one-sided affair as the Ryder Cup came to a wet, soggy Ligonier in a one-sided match that would help create the modern event we enjoy today.

CHAPTER 23

1975: A SUPER BOWL MALAISE...UM, NO

THE STEELERS GO BACK-TO-BACK

By David Finoli

Both Bill Cowher and Mike Tomlin can attest to the fact that some teams go through a malaise after winning the Super Bowl, playing substandard football and not putting in the effort that is needed to stay on top. After an impressive playoff run in 1974, especially from their stout defense, that gave the Pittsburgh Steelers their first Super Bowl championship, it wouldn't have stunned many to see them go a little in reverse the following season. Legendary teams don't allow that to happen. Instead of falling off the next season, Chuck Noll's young squad took what they learned in winning a championship and became even better. They took their title-winning team and became a squad that was even more dominant a year later on their way to winning another championship.

While the season ended up being the finest in franchise history to that date, it may have started out with the team wondering if it was in a malaise. After finishing undefeated in the preseason the year before, the Steelers were a bit sluggish in 1975, with a 3–4 preseason mark. That was all forgotten a week later when the team traveled to San Diego to open up the official defense of their crown in the regular season opener. The defense continued where it left off, holding the Charger offense to only 146 total yards while the explosive, balanced offense netted 443 (205 rushing, 238 passing) in a one-sided 37–0 victory. They hosted Buffalo a week later, the same Bills team they manhandled in the first round of the playoffs in 1974, 32–14. While most figured the Steelers would have little trouble at home in this rematch, a

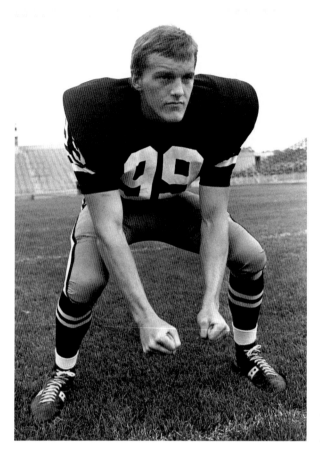

When the Steelers drafted Jack Lambert in the second round of the 1974 NFL draft, he was an undersized linebacker out of Kent State. He went on to compensate for his lack of size with a tough attitude that made him one of the greatest linebackers ever to take the field. *Photo courtesy of Kent State Athletics.*

funny thing happened to their potential 2–0 start: the formidable Pittsburgh defense met the real O.J. Simpson.

Somehow Pittsburgh couldn't stop the man they called "the Juice." He blistered what was an impenetrable Pittsburgh front line to the tune of 227 yards, a record at the time against a Pittsburgh team that included a magnificent 88-yard touchdown run in the third quarter that gave Buffalo a 23–0 lead. The play came as Pittsburgh was loading the front in an effort to stop Simpson when quarterback Joe Ferguson called a sweep right. Joe Greene was thoroughly impressed with Simpson. In a *Pittsburgh Post-Gazette* article, he said, "They talk a lot about Buffalo's offensive line and they can keep talking about the line, but it's the Juice who makes the difference, not the line, the Juice."

With the Steelers struggling, Noll inserted Joe Gilliam into the lineup to replace an ineffective Terry Bradshaw. Gilliam had a fine game throwing for

200 second-half yards to make the final a more respectable 30–21 loss, but the fans and players alike were wondering: What happened? Was the team just not as good this year? Their question would be quickly answered over the next few weeks.

Pittsburgh was pissed, and their rivals the Cleveland Browns would see just how pissed they were. Bradshaw started and was magnificent until he cut his finger after hitting it on a facemask. Joe Gilliam was equally as magnificent, until he dislocated his finger. The Steelers offense as a whole amassed 501 total yards, with the defense, led by Greene—who was ejected in the second quarter after getting into a fight—only allowing 221 yards, less than Simpson ran for the week before. The final outcome was a 42–6 win, and the Steelers never looked back.

It was the beginning of an 11-game winning streak during which the team was rarely challenged. With the exception of a Roy Gerela field goal with under two minutes left that beat the Packers 16–13 and a fourth-quarter 21-yard pass from Bradshaw to John Stallworth for a touchdown that gave Pittsburgh a 24–17 victory over the Houston Oilers, the team was rarely challenged as they brought a 12–1 mark into the final contest of the year at Los Angeles against the Rams. It was a meaningless game, and the team played like they knew it in a very lackluster 10–3 loss where they turned the ball over four times. Despite the turnovers, Franco Harris had a wonderful contest running for 126 yards while setting the franchise's all-time record for rushing yards in a season with 1,246.

With a 12–2 season behind them that included their third Central Division crown in four years, they were out to prove the Rams defeat was nothing more than an outlying poor performance in a magnificent campaign as they faced the Baltimore Colts in the first round of the playoffs at Three Rivers Stadium. It looked like the team could possibly still be in a malaise after the Colts took a 10–7 lead early in the third quarter as Pittsburgh was once again turning the ball over with four more in this contest. That's when the Steelers defense took over as it had done in the postseason the year before. After a Rocky Bleier touchdown put them ahead 14–10 in the third, Bradshaw took one in from two yards out, and the old man of the defense Andy Russell picked up a fumble as the Colts were driving to cut into the Steeler lead and rambled 93 yards to put the game out of reach 28–10.

The next week, they once again were taking on the Oakland Raiders in the AFC Championship game, the fourth year in a row they faced the Raiders in the postseason. It was a cold, blustery day at Three Rivers Stadium. The field was a sheet of ice, especially near the sidelines, with the explanation being that the team put tarp over the field and an icy rain came down overnight, leaking through the tarp onto the field. Raider owner Al Davis thought the team did it intentionally as the temperature dipped to 18 degrees. It was a closely fought game in adverse conditions as the two teams combined for 13 turnovers, with the Steelers amassing eight, three of which came on fumbles in the last five minutes of the game.

After the Steelers took what seemed like an insurmountable 16–7 lead following a Bradshaw-to-Stallworth connection for a 20-yard touchdown pass, Youngwood's George Blanda kicked a late 41-yard field goal to bring Oakland to within six at 16–10. With time running out, the Raiders secured the onside kick, but Oakland just didn't have enough time to score as the game ended with Cliff Branch catching a ball in Steeler territory.

The games in the 1975 postseason were much closer than the year before, and when the Steelers took on the Dallas Cowboys in Miami at Super Bowl X, they found themselves down 10–7 going into the final quarter. Receiver Lynn Swann was having a magnificent day, making what is still considered some of the most acrobatic catches in the game's history. After Reggie Harrison blocked a punt out of the end zone for a safety and Roy Gerela kicked two field goals, Pittsburgh had a 15–10 lead. It was then that Bradshaw hit Swann on a 64-yard touchdown that seemingly put the game out of reach 21–10. For Swann, it was his fourth catch for 161 yards; for Bradshaw, he was crushed after tossing the pass and was out of the game. The Cowboys cut the lead to four, 21–17, on an 80-yard drive, then took over late in the game when the Steelers went for it on fourth down and failed at the Dallas 39. Roger Staubach led the Cowboys to the Steelers 38 with seconds left, but an interception by Glen Edwards on the final play of the contest sealed Pittsburgh's second consecutive Super Bowl championship. It was a season that began as if the Steelers had a Super Bowl malaise and ended with them becoming one of the greatest teams in NFL history.

CHAPTER 24

1975: A LOSS OF HISTORIC PROPORTIONS

THE PENGUINS BLOW AN UNBLOWABLE LEAD

By David Finoli

There are two distinctly different portions of Pittsburgh Penguins history: one coming after 1991, where they were one of the most successful franchises in the annals of the NHL, capturing five Stanley Cups, and one before 1991, when if something could go wrong, it would. In 1975, the Pens' ability to embarrass themselves was on display as they were finishing what would be the most successful season the team had ever enjoyed to that point—and would enjoy until the Stanley Cup era. They amassed 89 points that year. Not a season for the ages, to be sure, but for this struggling franchise, it showed a potential light at the end of the tunnel for their championship dreams. It was a young team with incredible offensive potential, one that seemed like it was easily headed to NHL's Final Four— that is, until they wanted to make history, history of epic proportions, to be sure, just not history that anyone would want to make.

To this point, only one team in NHL history had blown a three-games-to-none lead in the playoffs: the 1942 Detroit Red Wings, who succumbed to the Toronto Maple Leafs after building such an insurmountable lead. Hell, in the history of major professional sports in North America, that was the only time it had ever happened. That is, until the Pittsburgh Penguins said, "Hold my beer," and quickly derailed their championship hopes against a young underdog New York Islanders team.

To be fair, this was the beginning of what turned out to be a team for the ages, as the Isles would go on to win four consecutive Stanley Cups in the

In 1975, one of the biggest surprises for the Pittsburgh Penguins was the emergence of their young rookie star Pierre Larouche. He would score 31 goals that season for the Pens but couldn't save them from one of the biggest collapses in NHL history as they blew a three-games-to-none lead against the New York Islanders. *Photo courtesy of the QMJHL.*

not-too-distant future; it's just that no one knew it at the time, certainly not this young Penguin team.

While 89 points might seem like nothing more than an average season in today's NHL, back in the '70s, when men were men and tied games actually ended in a tie, 89 points was considered a decent season. For Penguin fans, decent was more than they had ever imagined. It was a very talented and deep offensive team that boasted nine 20-goal scorers and was fourth in the league in scoring with 326 goals. They were led by the franchise's first great scorer, Jean Pronovost, with 43 goals. They also had veteran former New York Ranger great Vic Hadfield (31 goals); centers Ron Schock (23) and Syl Apps (24), the player who was the leading all-time scorer for the franchise before a man named Mario Lemieux came along; Rick Kehoe (32); sniper Lowell MacDonald (27); the rifleman Chuck Arnason (26); toughman Bob "Battleship" Kelly, who was more known for his fists, having scored only 16 goals in two NHL seasons prior to 1974–75 (27); and the team's first-round draft pick, a 19-year-old from Taschereau, Quebec, who set the Quebec Junior Hockey League on fire with a record 251 points for Sorel in only 67 games by the name of Pierre Larouche. The plan was to start "Lucky Pierre" in the minors to get him some seasoning, but he was so impressive the Pens had no choice but to keep him with the parent team. He went on to score 31 goals and was named Rookie of the Year by both the *Hockey News* and the *Sporting News*.

The team also had a tough defense led by Ron Stackhouse and Dave Burrows and a second-year 25-year-old goalie, Gary Inness, who had a solid season with a 24–18–10 record and 3.10 goals against average to go with a .905 save percentage.

Coach Marc Boileau led the team to a third-place finish in the Norris Division and a spot in the postseason with a first-round matchup against the

St. Louis Blues in a best-of-three game series. Game one didn't start out well as the Blues scored two first-period goals to go up 2–0 and led 3–1 early in the third. The Pens battled back as Arnason scored two in the final period to tie the contest and Larouche scored his first postseason goal with only 2:31 left in regulation to give Pittsburgh a dramatic 4–3 win. Two nights later, the series shifted to St. Louis, where the Blues once again were leading; this time, it was 3–2 in the second before Syl Apps tied it on a power play goal late in the period. Defenseman Colin Campbell and Hadfield netted third-period goals to give the Penguins the 5–3 win and the franchise's first series victory. With the win, coupled with upset victories by Chicago over the Bruins and Toronto against the Los Angeles Kings, the Pens had a surprising home-ice advantage in the next round and were to face the upstart New York Islanders in the quarter final round.

The Isles were also in the midst of the first good season in the franchise's history, finishing a point behind the Pens with 88, and pulled off a win in the first round against their hated rivals, the New York Rangers, whom they defeated in the third and final game 4–3 in overtime with a J.P. Parise goal. Even though the Islanders were talented, they looked overmatched against the Penguins, losing the first three contests 5–4, 4–3 and 6–4. After five consecutive postseason wins, Pittsburgh seemed like they were on their way to the final four as it finally seemed this team would join the Pirates and Steelers with a successful run in the playoffs. As was stated earlier in the chapter, only one team in the history of major sports in North America ever blew a three-games-to-none lead in a playoff series. Move over 1942 Red Wings, because it was at this point the Pens became the Pens and would join them in the history books.

At the Nassau Coliseum in game four, Kelly tied it at one in the second period, and hopes in Pittsburgh were high that the series would be over before the night was done. The Islander defense began to smother the Pens offense while New York scored twice in a 49-second span to give the home team life in the series and a 3–1 victory. Pittsburgh peppered goalie Glenn "Chico" Resch with 38 shots in game five while allowing only 19 to the Islanders, but Resch was at his best as the Isles were able to build a 3–1 lead. MacDonald gave the Pens hope with a third period goal, but Jude Drouin netted an empty netter to bring New York back from the dead and force a game six.

After a scoreless first period, the Islander went up 1–0 in the second before Larouche tied it 49 seconds later. That was it for the visitors as the Isles dominated the rest of the game, giving them a 4–1 victory that evaporated the once-insurmountable Penguin advantage. There would now, remarkably, be a game seven that no one thought they'd see. It would be at the Civic Arena as a sellout crowd of 13,404 was hoping to will the Penguins to victory. The home team seemed to dominate play and would outshoot New York 30–17, including a 25–11 advantage in the first two periods. Unfortunately, they were going up against Resch, who was now impenetrable, as the two teams went into this thrilling contest scoreless after two. For most of the game, they would be without Hadfield, who tried to play despite the fact he had broken two ribs in game six.

Larouche looked like he was going to put Pittsburgh up 1–0, and he broke in on the young New York netminder but only got off a weak shot. With only 3:38 left in regulation, Ed Westfall scored the goal that put a knife in the Penguins' back and a 1–0 win that completed the historic comeback. Pittsburgh had nothing left and no shots on goal after that. Hall of Fame coach Al Arbour was glowing after the game. "We were written off when we were down by three games. This team doesn't know what the word quit means," he said in a *Pittsburgh Press* article after the game. A bewildered Boileau just quipped, "We got overconfident…definitely."

The season was now over as the Pens joined a historic list they didn't want to be part of: teams that blew a three-games-to-none lead in a series. Instead of using this season as a steppingstone to greater things, this was the highwater mark for the Pittsburgh Penguins until being saved by Mario Lemieux over a decade later. By June, it was revealed that the franchise was in dire financial shape as the IRS padlocked the Civic Arena doors until the team found $6 million to satisfy its debts. Even though Edward DeBartolo Sr. would eventually give them a lifeline a year later, it was just another slap in the face for a Penguin franchise that seemed to find itself always on the short end of the stick.

CHAPTER 25

1975: EAST DIVISION DOMINANCE

THE PIRATES CAPTURE THEIR FIFTH DIVISION TITLE OF THE '70s

By David Finoli

When fans look at the current state of Pittsburgh Pirate baseball, generally, the last thing they look forward to is the club competing for a division championship, much less winning one. Almost fifty years ago, it was a different story. Winning the Eastern Division was something patrons not only just hoped for but expected. After finishing below .500 during a season where the team grieved the loss of their leader and hero Roberto Clemente in 1973, the Bucs recaptured the eastern crown a year later. In 1975, it was a mixture of veterans and youth as they would push for a fifth title in six seasons.

While they had been winning for the majority of the first half of the decade, they were still relatively a young team with only Willie Stargell and Manny Sanguillen being over 30 years old when it came to the regulars. Stargell, who had been in left field for most of his career at this point, moved to first base. Pirate management had thought slugger Bob Robertson would be the man who would hold the position at first, but Robertson had knee issues for most of the prior season, necessitating an operation on both. Coming off three successive poor seasons at the plate, partially due to his injuries, Bob was relegated to backup status behind the 35-year-old future Hall of Famer. Stargell made the most of his time at first, hitting .295 with 22 homers and 90 RBIs. He also was felled by injuries during the season, missing 18 games after fracturing a rib in late August.

In 1975, John Candelaria was a rookie pitcher who quickly became one of the best the Pittsburgh Pirates had to offer. He went 8–6 that season with a 2.76 ERA and then saved his best for last, striking out what was then a NLCS-record 14 batters in game three against the Reds. *Photo courtesy of the Pittsburgh Pirates.*

If Stargell and second baseman Rennie Stennett, who hit .286, were the highlights of the infield, shortstop Frank Taveras and third baseman Richie Hebner were the opposite. Hebner did show some power with 15 home runs, but hit only .246, a career low by 25 points, while Taveras hit a miniscule .212, stealing only 17 bases. As poorly as the Bucs shortstop played, the team didn't have many options to replace him with Mario Mendoza (.180) and Craig Reynolds (.224) as his backups.

With the infield questionable on the left side, the outfield was one of the best in the game, at least offensively. Left fielder Richie Zisk hit under .300 for the first time in his career as a regular at .290 but slugged a career high 20 homers. Veteran center fielder Al "Scoops" Oliver, who was in his seventh season with the club, hit .280 while also showing decent power with 18 homers, the second highest of his career at that point. In right, the Bucs finally had an All-Star replacement for the late Roberto Clemente. In his first season as a regular, Dave Parker showed the massive potential that many knew he had. The 24-year-old led the league in slugging at .541, was second in triples (10) and fifth in both homers (25) and RBIs (101), hitting an 11th best .308.

With their offense as potent as it had been throughout most of the decade, the impressive thing about the team in 1975 was its pitching staff, which finished second in the league with a 3.01 ERA. Lefty's Jerry Reuss, 18–11–2.54 ERA, and Jim Rooker, 13–11–2.97, led the way, with Bruce Kison, 12–11–3.23, Dock Ellis, 8–9–3.79, and Ken Brett, 9–5–3.36, rounding out a solid rotation. After the season, the controversial Ellis and Brett were dealt to the New York Yankees with Willie Randolph for Pitt grad George "Doc" Medich—not one of general manager Joe L. Brown's finest trades.

Oh yeah, I think there was one other pitcher that had a decent season. It was 21-year-old rookie left-hander John Candelaria, who began his long major league career on June 6 and went 8–6 with a fine 2.75 ERA.

The bullpen was led by men who had been constants over the decade as Dave Giusti had 17 saves, Ramón Hernández won seven games with a 2.95 ERA and the man who would eventually take over for Giusti as the closer, Kent Tekulve, made his major league call-up permanent after coming from AAA Charleston and had an impressive 2.25 ERA, giving up only 43 hits in 56 innings pitched.

It was a solid club, but they got off to a very slow start, sitting at only 18–18 by May 24 in fourth place. They then went on a six-game winning streak, and after defeating the San Francisco Giants 7–6 on June 7—thanks to a Hebner home run in the top of the eighth inning to tie the contest and a sacrifice fly by Sanguillen, which scored Mendoza to put them ahead—the Bucs took over first place by themselves and never relinquished it the rest of the season.

The Bucs had built a 4½-game lead by August 5 after a 6–1 victory over the Cardinals and stood 66–44. It was at that point that the season almost slipped away. The Bucs suddenly forgot how to score and lost 11 of their next 12 games, defeating only Atlanta 8–1 on August 11, a win that was

PITTSBURGH SPORTS IN THE 1970s

sandwiched in between a five-game losing streak and a six-game one. They had scored only 22 runs in the 11 losses, and their 4½-game lead had been reduced to a mere half game with the young Phillies now precariously close to taking over the top spot that they eventually would hold on to between 1976 and 1978.

Manager Danny Murtaugh was a veteran and wouldn't let the team fall any further. Pittsburgh then won seven of their next eight games and, by the beginning of September, built their lead back up to four games after Stennett had three hits and Robertson showed some of his old power with his sixth homer of the year in a 9–6 win over the Astros. The race was all but over at that time as they built their advantage to eight games with a 3–1 win over the Phils on September 23, then finished 92–69, winning the East by 6½.

Unfortunately, until they exorcised their demons in the 1979 NLCS, they never beat the Cincinnati Reds in the postseason, losing the 1970 and 1972 NLCS to their rivals. They were going up against arguably the strongest team in the 1970s and one of the strongest in the history of the game, the Big Red Machine, in 1975, and once again, they would go down. The Bucs showed they weren't in the Reds' class, losing the first two games 8–3 and 6–1. In the final contest in the best-of-five series, Candelaria had a game for the ages, striking out a then NLCS record 14 batters in 7⅔ innings as the Pirates tied the score 3–3 in the bottom of the ninth when Rawley Eastwick walked Duffy Dyer with the bases loaded. Ed Armbrister knocked in Ken Griffey Sr. with a sacrifice fly and Joe Morgan doubled in Pete Rose off of Hernández to put the final touches on a Cincinnati sweep with a 5–3 win.

While the dominance the Pirates had over the Eastern Division would end in 1975, their impressive five titles in six seasons truly made them the kings of the East at this point.

128

CHAPTER 26

1975: COLORED COURTS, WEIRD SCORING AND TWO HEARTTHROBS

THE TRIANGLES ARE THE BEST OF THE WTT

By David Finoli

I'm not going to kid you. The 1970s were mostly about the success of the Pirates and Steelers. Yeah, there was the occasional team that won a title we didn't expect (e.g., the Pitt Panthers capturing the 1976 national championship), but most fans had their eyes firmly placed on those two franchises. In 1974, another franchise was introduced to the Steel City: the Pittsburgh Triangles. It was a tennis team—yeah, team tennis. That in itself was weird enough. I know that team tennis was a Davis Cup thing, but let's face it, in a hard-nosed town like Pittsburgh, not many sports fans paid attention to Davis Cup tennis. The league was called World Team Tennis (WTT), and the courts had funky colors. To make matters even more confusing, traditional tennis scoring—15, 30, 45 and then game—was replaced by 1, 2, 3 and 4 with no ties, or "AD," as the tennis world called a lead that wasn't by two points if players got past a 45–45 tie. (Well, I guess the tradition was more confusing and the WTT made it easier, but it was different.) The team score was also simple: win a game in the set, win a point for your team. Hell, the sport was even invented in the Steel City in 1973 when Chuck Reichblum was among a group that conceived the concept here. How could the Triangles ever hope to survive? By signing two heartthrobs, Vitas Gerulaitis and Evonne Goolagong Cawley. It was a marketing concept that no other franchise in the city could match.

Not only was Goolagong Cawley stealing the hearts of many Pittsburghers, but she was also a kickass tennis player who was destroying most female tennis players on the court. An Australian Aborigine, Evonne burst onto the tennis scene at 19 years old in 1971 when she captured the singles titles at both Wimbledon and the French Open. She went on to win a second title at Wimbledon in 1980 while also raising the trophy at the Australian Open four times. At Flushing Meadows in the U.S. Open, she would reach the finals in consecutive years between 1973 and 1976 but, unfortunately, never emerged victorious. All told, including her doubles titles, she won 13 grand slam championships, was number one in the world at the end of the 1971 season and in April 1976 and won 86 single titles in her career on tour. So when she came to play for the Triangles in 1974, it was a very big deal and helped set up the team for the early success it enjoyed.

Gerulaitis was not as successful as Evonne, but he was every bit as popular in the Steel City, if not more. He was only 20 years old when he came to Pittsburgh in 1974 and eventually would add two grand slam titles to his résumé: the Australian Open singles championship in 1977 and doubles at Wimbledon in 1975. He tragically died of carbon monoxide poisoning in 1994. In the mid-'70s, he was king of the Burgh. In an article in the *Pittsburgh Post-Gazette*, sportswriter and talk show host Mark Madden recalled, "Gerulaitis may have been the most popular Triangle. A group of Gerulaitis fans called the G-Men noisily filled several rows of seats at home matches. Gerulaitis often hosted postmatch parties at his residence. Open to the public."

Besides the two leaders, coach Vic Edwards—who was Goolagong's personal coach and was elevated to the Triangles' head spot after their original coach, Hall of Famer Ken Rosewall, was fired following a successful first season with the team—had at his disposal Rayni Fox, who went to the doubles final at the French Open in 1977; Peggy Michel, who won two Australian Opens and a Wimbledon doubles title with Goolagong Cawley; Mark Cox, who advanced to the quarterfinals in the Australian Open twice and the U.S. Open on one occasion; and Kim Warwick, who had six Grand Slam doubles championships, including the 1972 Australian Open mixed doubles title with his now-teammate Evonne Goolagong Cawley.

The team was owned by a man who was a legend in the Pittsburgh sports world over the years by the name of Frank Fuhrer. Madden remembered Fuhrer, owner of a successful beer distributorship, as a man who intensely wanted to win. "Fuhrer ran the Triangles (and also indoor soccer's Spirit) with ruthless efficiency. Many dream about Mark Cuban owning the Pirates.

I'd choose Fuhrer. Fuhrer badly wanted to win and made sure that desire trickled down." That desire did trickle down to the point where the team went 36–8, winning the Eastern Division regular season crown.

In the playoffs, the Triangles faced the Boston Lobsters in a best-of-three series to see who would represent the East in the WTT finals. It wasn't much of a contest, as Pittsburgh easily won the two matches 23–16 and 23–14. Their opponents in the finals would be a team from San Francisco called the Golden Gaters, and after Pittsburgh blew a 24–20 lead in game one going into the final set when Betty Stove and player/coach Fred McMillan crushed Warwick and Michel 6–1 in mixed doubles, giving San Francisco a 26–25 victory, the Triangles knew they had no margin for error if they wanted to hoist the Bancroft Trophy.

The Triangles pulled off a 28–25 win in game two, sending the series to a third and decisive match at the Civic Arena. A large WTT crowd of 6,882 entered the arena. Fuhrer came in with a G-Man T-shirt on. After Goolagong Cawley and Michel lost the opening set 6–2, Pittsburgh took control. A frustrated Goolagong Cawley crushed Stove 6–2 to tie the match, and after Gerulaitis and Cox nipped McMillan and Tom Okker 7–5, they had a 15–13 lead with the G-Man heading into a men's singles match against Okker. Gerulaitis was at his best, embarrassing Okker 6–1. He was so dominant that Okker tossed his racquet into the crowd at one point out of frustration. The one-sided win gave Pittsburgh an insurmountable 21–14 lead, making the mixed doubles match unnecessary and giving the Triangles their championship.

Instead of the beginning of a bright future, 1975 was pretty much it for the franchise. The 1976 campaign was forgettable, as Goolagong Cawley became pregnant and was unable to compete. Fuhrer folded the club following the season. The league tried to keep the Pittsburgh market by first creating a team called the Pittsburgh Keystones, which would be a Philadelphia/Pittsburgh amalgamation playing half its games in each city. When that didn't work—they folded before the season began—the WTT decided to play half of the Cleveland Nets games at the Civic Arena. Pittsburgh rooting for a Cleveland team? That had failure written all over it.

So in the end, the WTT left the Steel City, never to return, but for one season, they had the best team the league had to offer—and one that is still fondly remembered by those who experienced the joy that was 1975 Pittsburgh Triangle tennis.

CHAPTER 27

1975: *SLAP SHOT* IN REAL LIFE

THE JOHNSTOWN JETS WIN A CHAMPIONSHIP

By David Finoli

When it comes to hockey cinema, arguably the greatest movie ever written about the sport starred Paul Newman and went by the name of *Slap Shot*. It had everything. *Slap Shot* is the story of a minor league club called the Charlestown Chiefs in a city that is laying off thousands of workers at a steel mill. Faced with a financial crisis, they resort to violence on the ice and end up winning the league title. Hell, it even has a love story that stars the mother in *A Christmas Story* as Newman's female counterpart. Wow—talk about acting on two completely different spectrums. Now the movie has gone on to incredible cult status, as is told wonderfully in chapter 41 of this book by Tom Rooney, so that's all we will say about *Slap Shot*. Except—somehow, it had to be inspired by something. That inspiration was a real minor league team by the name of the Johnstown Jets, which existed in some form or another for 27 years between 1950 and 1977, winning six league championships, including their final one in 1975, when they captured the North American Hockey League title.

For the Jets, this season truly was life imitating art. There was a player on the Jets by the name of Ned Dowd. He was a left wing that was mostly forgettable, with 10 goals and 26 points in 43 games. His one lasting contribution was his sister, a writer, who followed the team and ended up writing a screenplay, which, of course, was for *Slap Shot*. She had an incredible story to develop through this team's contributions. There was a trio of brothers that skated for the team called the Carlson brothers—just

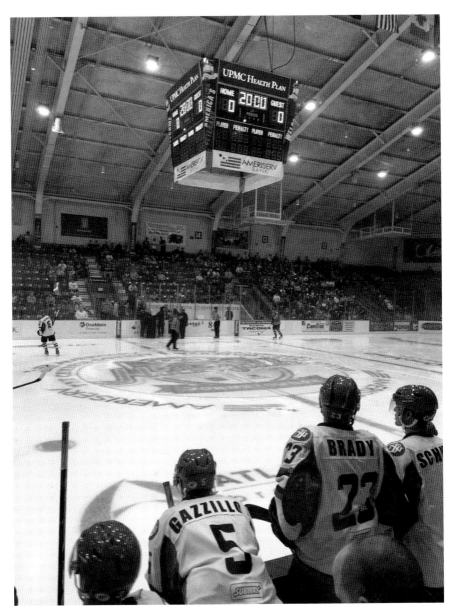

The ice surface at the First Summit Arena in Johnstown. In 1975, the facility was known simply as the Cambria County War Memorial Arena and played host to the 1975 NAHL Champion Johnstown Jets. *Photo courtesy of David Finoli.*

like the movie's legendary trio named the Hansons. Steve, a 19-year-old wing who led the team with 30 goals and 88 points, was combined with his brothers, Jack (27 goals) and Jeff (15), to form the Carlson brother line. While Steve was the talent offensively, Jack and Jeff also provided brawn with 246 and 250 penalty minutes respectively. Steve and Jeff would portray Jack and Jeff Hanson in the movie, while Jack—who was called up to Minnesota in the World Hockey Association, eventually securing a spot in the NHL with Minnesota and St Louis—was left out of *Slap Shot*. The third Hanson brother in the movie was also played by a Jet, tough defenseman who had the correct last name, Dave Hanson. The 20-year-old had 10 goals for the club but, more importantly, contributed 249 minutes in the penalty box. As I said, it truly was life imitating art.

Over the years, the Jets were one of the most successful minor league franchises in the game. In the old Eastern Hockey League, they captured five championships between 1951 and 1961 and produced 46 players that ended up in the National Hockey League, including former Penguin general manager and coach Eddie Johnston. When the 1974–75 version of the franchise, which had moved to the NAHL in 1973, began the season, hope of a sixth title seemed to be remote. The club was emphasizing its toughness, even running an ad campaign that said, "Aggressive hockey is back in Johnstown," and they weren't kidding: the team combined for 1,601 penalty minutes. The problem was that aggressive hockey wasn't working at first. The team stood at 15–24–4 by January 18, and a .500 season looked like a long shot, much less qualifying for the playoffs. Eventually, Coach Dick Roberge, who was a Jet legend eventually given the honor of having his number retired, got them to win. They won 25 of their final 31 contests to finish in fourth place with a 38–32–4 mark, securing a playoff spot and a matchup with Cape Codders in the first round. In an article in the *Tribune-Democrat*, Steve Carlson remembered, "We started playing as a team, Dick had us playing together. We were a tough team. We would go in there and not only beat them on the scoreboard, we actually beat them physically on the ice"—yes, once again, life imitating art. Roberge said, "It was a combination of desire with the guys and everything came together, really. I don't know how we did it. Everybody really hung in there and fought real well. It was extraordinary."

They defeated the Codders three games to one in the best-of-five series and took on a more difficult opponent in the semifinals, the Syracuse Blazers. The Blazers were the best team in the league with 95 points and were 32–5 at home. To make matters worse, the Jets hadn't won in Syracuse in 41 contests

The memorial outside of the First Summit Arena in Johnstown that is dedicated to those from Cambria County who gave their lives in defense of the country. *Photo courtesy of David Finoli.*

that dated back to 1970. The teams each won their contests over the first six games at home, setting up a game seven at the Syracuse War Memorial Auditorium, where the Blazers were the prohibitive favorites. It was a game that more than met the anticipation and made this special season even more so for the Jets. It also looked a lot like the movie the team inspired at the end. An enthusiastic crowd of 3,407 came into the 6,000-seat arena and were treated to a classic. Syracuse outshot the Jets 37–22 in the first two periods and was up 1–0 after one. Despite being outshot in the second, Johnstown scored three unanswered goals with John Tetreault knocking one in from 40 feet out before Carlson put them up 2–1 1:25 later. The Jets made it 3–1 when John Campigotto tipped in a Vern Campbell shot. Syracuse scored 27 seconds later, but when Mike Chernoff sent a 22-foot shorthanded shot past the Blazers goalie with Hanson in the penalty box, the Jets' two-goal lead was restored.

Syracuse wasn't done, with two goals in 1:41 late in the second to tie the game at four going into the final period. Blowing a two-goal lead and not winning in this building in 41 attempts—to say the Blazers were the favorites to pull this out was an understatement. The Jets were not going to let that happen. They played their best hockey of the game, outshooting Syracuse 20–8. When Carlson scored his second goal of the game with only 3:09 remaining in the contest to give the Jets a 5–4 advantage, the team became even more inspired. They thoroughly dominated the final minutes, forcing a Blazer penalty with only 1:48 left to end the winless streak and send Johnstown to the finals.

The place went crazy after the unexpected loss. The fans began to storm the ice and chased referee Brendan Watson. They caught him as he was trying to escape through a door, and he suffered a head laceration as he fell and some bruises from punches the fans threw before they were pulled off. It was a scene certainly meant for a movie such as *Slap Shot*. Roberge was ecstatic. In an article in the Syracuse *Post-Standard* following the dramatic win, he said, "One of my biggest thrills in hockey. It means an awful lot of money to us. We'll pack them in for the finals against the Dusters."

The Dusters were the Broom County Dusters from Binghamton, New York, and after defeating the best team in the league, the Dusters had no chance to take the series from the Jets. Roberge remembered, "Thinking back, the big game was in Syracuse for Game 7. When we walked away winning that, it really boosted them up.

"Nobody could touch us after that in the playoffs."

Nobody could. After a 10-day delay to start the finals due to an already scheduled home show, an art festival in Johnstown and a circus in Binghamton, the Jets swept through the first three games of the series 6–1, 7–4 and 2–1 before returning to the War Memorial in Johnstown for game four. The Jets were greeted by a sellout crowd of 4,088 enthusiastic fans, and there was no way the team was going to let this one go beyond four games. They outshot the Dusters in the first 20–9 and scored three goals from John Gofton, Reg Bechtold and Mike Chernoff to end the first period up 3–0. Things were no better for the visitors in the second after captain Gaelen Head scored twice and Jeff Carlson knocked in an unassisted goal at 9:01 to extend their advantage to 6–0.

The visitors managed two goals in the final period and a half but never came close to victory as Johnstown closed out the series and captured the Lockhart Cup with a 6–2 victory. They tried to parade the cup around the ice, but as in the movie, the fans stormed onto the ice in a wild celebration. Head recalled the incredible crowd. "I played before some very good crowds in Johnstown, that night it seemed as if people were hanging off the rafters watching us play that game." Roberge, who resigned after the game, said, "I don't know how we did it. Everybody really hung in there and fought real well. It was extraordinary."

It truly was extraordinary, giving not only Johnstown its last hockey championship to date but also hockey fans everywhere an unbelievable screenplay that they can enjoy in perpetuity.

CHAPTER 28

1975: THE BIRTH OF
THE TERRIBLE TOWEL

By David Finoli

In chapter 2, we touch briefly on the flag of the Pittsburgh Steeler Nation, the Terrible Towel, but we were writing more about the greatness of its creator, Myron Cope, and his journey that made him an icon among Western Pennsylvania sports fans who had the honor of listening to him on the radio and TV on a nightly basis. This chapter deals specifically with his greatest gift to Steeler fans: the Terrible Towel, of course, and what it has meant to them over the years. It's their flag that tells the world that they are die-hard Pittsburgh Steelers fans, a symbol that no one who roots for the black and gold is without.

The Terrible Towel has become something so important to the area that we will tell the story of its invention once again. It was 1975, and the Steelers were about to embark on the postseason in an effort to defend the Super Bowl title they had won the year before. In their first forty years of existence, they had won absolutely nothing: no division titles, no world championships, nothing at all. During the first few years of the 1970s, that all changed with the 1972 Central Division and the ensuing Immaculate Reception victory over the Raiders in their first postseason game in 25 years. They now counted three division titles and a world championship on their résumé and desperately wanted more. Cope's contract was running out, and the powers that be at the team's flagship station, which Myron worked for, WTAE-AM, were putting pressure on him to come up with a gimmick for their home playoff game against the Baltimore Colts, insinuating that if it was

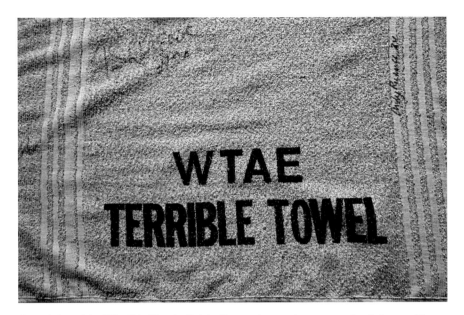

One of the original Terrible Towels. Originally, people were just supposed to bring a gold towel from home to root for the Steelers. When this became incredibly popular, official towels were produced. Today, proceeds from sales of the towel go to the Allegheny Valley School in Coraopolis, a school that cares for people with intellectual and physical disabilities. It has raised more than $6 million to date for the facility. *Photo courtesy of David Finoli.*

successful, it might give him leverage in his upcoming contract negotiation. Many things were discussed, including a black mask they could give out to fans with coach Chuck Noll's motto, "Whatever it takes," on it. A Terrible Mask?! Luckily, that idea was quickly shot down.

In the past, the team sold cowbells at the stadium that fans could ring during the game, but this was not something they were looking for, either. Vice president for sales Larry Garrett then chimed in, "How about towels?" The suggestion got Myron's juices flowing immediately. In his book *Double Yoi!*, he states, "A towel? Yes we could call it the Terrible Towel. And I could go on radio and television proclaiming 'The Terrible Towel is poised to strike!'" When someone else in the room said, "Yes, black and gold towels," Cope immediately shot that down. "No. Black ones won't provide color. We'll tell them to bring gold or yellow towels. I'll tell them they can use the towels to wipe their seats clean. They can use it as a muffler against the cold. They can drape it over their heads if it rains." But whatever fans wanted to do with it, it was something they could get at their house for free and go nuts with at the game.

Cope promoted it aggressively, and as the game began on December 27, 1975, he was stunned as he looked out into the crowd and saw very few towels, perhaps a dozen at best. Fortunately, the fans had them tucked away, because when kickoff happened on this rainy day, the announcer approximated almost 30,000 towels appeared and were waving. The Terrible Towel had officially been born on this day and was a success. No one, though, could have even imagined what a success it would eventually become.

The Steelers won 28–10 in a game that included a 93-yard fumble return by the soon-to-be-retiring old man of the defense, Andy Russell. It had magical powers. I could feel it as I was waving a yellow hand towel that I took from our hall closet for the contest. Tim Brown was also at that first game and recalled, "I was at the Colts playoff game with my mother's yellow towel. Andy Russell ran 93 yards with a fumble towards me for the clinching touchdown." Its magic then took the Steelers to a frigid win in the AFC Championship the next week against Oakland and then a Super Bowl X title versus the Cowboys. It was a game that my dad and mom attended. When they got home from Miami, my dad had quite a few souvenirs he gave us, including one of the Original Terrible Towels that WTAE had quickly printed up to give as travel gifts to some of the Pittsburghers that were in Miami for the week. Today, it remains one of my most treasured items.

While, originally, Cope only intended the Terrible Towel for special games, when the team really needed its magic for victory, it became something that Steeler fans brought to every game. Hey, the team needed daily magic, we all presumed. They started mass-producing them in 1978, as stores were regularly selling out of gold and yellow towels, and put the official Terrible Towel logo on them. Gimbels Department Store was the first to sell them at six dollars apiece and couldn't keep them in stock. The towel is one thing that inflation hasn't killed, as they go today currently for only 10 dollars.

Terrible Towels are sold everywhere—one million were sold before Super Bowl XLIII—and are done in special versions, such as Super Bowl versions, one honoring its inventor Cope when he retired and many others. The sales are plentiful, but Cope made sure that the profits would only go for good. In 1996, he gave the rights to the Allegheny Valley School in Coraopolis, a school his son Danny, who had severe autism, attended. It's a school that takes care of kids with intellectual and physical disabilities. Terrible Towel sales reportedly raised more than $6 million over the years for the school. No doubt the good the Terrible Towel does here adds to its magical qualities— and also curses those who disrespect it. Let me explain.

In 2005, after defeating the Steelers at Heinz Field to push them toward the division title, Cincinnati wide receiver T.J. Houshmandzadeh grabbed a Terrible Towel and wiped his shoes with it. Karma was not on the Bengals' side at that point, as they lost to Pittsburgh in the playoffs and Carson Palmer, their quarterback, was put out of action in the game. Yes, the Steelers went on to win the Super Bowl, and the Bengals lost for the next three years. After burning a towel before the 2016 opener, Washington would lose 38–16. Before a playoff game in 1994, the Browns' Earnest Byner stomped on a towel. The Browns lost 29–9 and were gone from Cleveland a couple years later. After defeating Pittsburgh in the 1994 AFC Championship game, the Chargers mockingly waved the towel. They were crushed in the Super Bowl by 23 points. In 2008, Phoenix mayor Phil Gordon blew his nose in the towel. The Cardinals ended up losing Super Bowl XLIII to Pittsburgh. Should I go on? Probably not; I think America now understands the power of the towel. Pittsburgh Steeler fans have also fallen in love with it and take it wherever they go.

Former Pittsburgher David Laza, who lives near Atlanta now, travels the globe and makes sure he gets a picture with the towel wherever he goes, as does Bedford's Mindy Bowling, who took it with her to both Jamaica and Iceland. Laza said,

> I love taking my Terrible Towel everywhere I travel, both in the US and to Europe. I have two towels, an original from 1975 and one I received as a gift several years back, and that's the one I travel with. It's been to Europe four times. My Dad and Mom used to share season tickets with their close friends. They bought the first towel for the 1975 playoffs, I believe they bought it at Horne's. I still have that original towel. I've lost Mom and Dad over the past few years and now that towel always makes me think of them and how blessed I have been in my life thanks to them. I watch every game with one of the Towels close by, and occasionally breakout a "yoi" or "double yoi" knowing yunz are all out there rooting our Steelers to victory. Other fan bases have tried to duplicate it, but there's only one Terrible Towel.

Fans would do whatever they had to in the early days to make sure they were Terrible Towel ready. James Marnell said that when he was a kid, "My twist on the Terrible Towel was for Super Bowl XIII. I spray-painted a WWII helmet black and used gold paint to spell 'The Terrible Helmet.' Still have it." Joe Magnu was unable to get one before the towel's first Super

Bowl. "They didn't make their way to Mercer County initially, so I made my own for Super Bowl X."

Through it all, the fans still understand the joy of the towel and what it means. Hell, just about every sport now has a towel of some sort, all starting with ours. For Daniel Haller Houston, a Steeler fan from the West Coast, it allowed him to feel more part of the Steeler Nation. "As someone who grew up on the West Coast, it meant a lot to me. My grandma mailed us one in 1978. It was something that connected us to Pittsburgh and a way we could participate even without being there." Ron Stefanacci puts its specialness in perspective. "Today, everyone is 'giving away' some kind of rag as a promotion. But today you have to buy your Terrible Towel, and this supports the charity of Myron Cope, the Allegheny Valley School. This is what separates the Terrible Towle from any other rag on the street."

It is truly special, an invention that no one could have predicted at the time how popular it would become. For Cope, it was his greatest contribution to Western Pennsylvania—and hopefully was a major plus in his 1975 contract negotiations.

CHAPTER 29

1976: THE CURSE
OF DANNY MURTAUGH

By David Finoli

I t was tough being a manager of the Pittsburgh Pirates in the 1960s and early 1970s. After all, being a manager in the major leagues is a tough enough venture without having a curse to deal with. Inevitably, if you were hired to manage the Bucs, you knew two things: your time was limited, and eventually, you'd be replaced by Danny Murtaugh. Three managers came in that period, and three were fired, only to be replaced by their predecessor. Finally, in 1975, the curse came to an end in a very unfortunate manner, when the man some consider the greatest to ever manage the team passed away at 59 on December 2, 1976.

Murtaugh had been a second baseman primarily with the Phillies and the Bucs in the 1940s, starting for Pittsburgh in 1948 and 1950 and leading the league in putouts in '48. After ending his major league career in 1951, he took over for the Pirates AA team in New Orleans as the manager before moving to their Charleston club in 1955. For most of the 1950s, Pittsburgh was the doormat of the National League. As the '50s were coming to an end, they seemed to have an array of young talent, but it just wasn't showing in the win/loss column. In 1957, manager Bobby Bragan was having difficulty developing that talent, as the team stood at a very disappointing 36–67. Young general manager Joe L. Brown let Bragan go at that point and wanted to give the job to first base coach Clyde Sukeforth. When the coach, who was more famous for signing Jackie Robinson as a Dodger scout, turned down

Casey Stengel (*left*) shakes the hand of Danny Murtaugh (*right*) before the 1960 World Series. Murtaugh went on to lead the Bucs to two world championships and is in the short discussion of greatest Pirate managers in the history of the franchise. *Photo courtesy of the Pittsburgh Pirates.*

the job, he recommended Murtaugh to Brown. Luckily, the GM listened to the veteran coach, as Danny turned the team into winners, finishing '57 with a 26–25 mark before leading the Bucs to a surprising second place finish a year later with an 84–70 record. Two years later, the Pirates upset the Yankees in the 1960 World Series to give the franchise their first world championship in 35 years. At that point, Danny Murtaugh went from short, pudgy manager to Pittsburgh icon—and eventually a curse to all managers that followed him. And now the curse is explained.

The Chester, Pennsylvania native kept the job through the 1964 season. He had learned he had a heart condition in 1962, and after two more years and two disappointing seasons, he decided to retire and move to the front office as a scout and advisor to Brown. The team hired Harry "the Hat" Walker, who led the club to two 90-plus winning seasons before stalling in 1967 as the Pirates stood at 42–42. Brown fired Walker and gave the job back to Danny to lead them the rest of the season. They went 39–39, but according to Andy Sturgill's biography on the manager for SABR.org, "Murtaugh admitted that he was not in the right frame of mind to manage and ended up serving more as a cheerleader on the bench than a real manager. Before the season ended the team announced that Murtaugh would not return as manager, and named him director of player acquisition and development, where he oversaw the farm system and scouting."

They would name Larry Shepard skipper, and he only survived two seasons. When Brown was looking to hire someone to take him into the 1970s, Murtaugh told him he was ready to take over full time again. After the general manager got assurances from Murtaugh's doctor that he could take over the job, Danny was at his best again, winning the Manager of the Year award following an Eastern Division crown in 1970 before leading the team to the world championship a year later. As fun as 1971 was on the field, the manager suffered from chest pains early in the season and retired once again following the World Series victory over the heavily favored Baltimore Orioles.

Pirate great Bill Virdon took over, and after a very successful 1972 campaign, the team struggled in 1973 following the tragic death of Roberto Clemente and limped in at the end with a disappointing 80–82 mark. Brown relieved Virdon of his job, and I'm sure at this point we know who the GM chose to replace him with. Murtaugh would right the ship and win division titles in both 1974 and 1975 before finishing his three-year run with a second place 92–70 finish in 1976. He retired once again at that point to spend more time with his family. As the Pirate Nation waited for Brown to name a manager, in the backs of their minds, they all figured somehow, some way, Murtaugh would eventually replace them—after all, he was only 59 years old and had been a curse to every other Pirate manager that preceded him. In early November, Brown went unconventional in looking for a replacement, trading popular catcher Manny Sanguillen and $100,000 to the Oakland A's for their manager, New Castle's own Chuck Tanner. Tanner was thrilled. As quoted in his biography on SABR.org, he exclaimed, "I can't wait for spring training. This is such a thrill. It's like a dream come true." It was a lot for the Bucs to give up, especially considering odds were Murtaugh would probably replace him in a year or two.

In late November, Danny went to a doctor's appointment and was given a clean bill of health. Unfortunately, the next day, he suffered a stroke and died a day later. *Pittsburgh Press* columnist Bob Smizik remembered him as a manager who may have been quiet, but, he said, "There was not a better baseball mind in the game. Other managers did not get a strategic leg up on Danny Murtaugh."

When he received the news, Brown was distraught. He was sobbing as he said, "I don't know the words. I haven't been close to as many men as I was to Danny. He was my very dear friend, and I said when he was alive he was like my brother. He was my brother. I loved him and I can't say any more than that. He was an unusual human being, a fine, fine fellow. I ache for his family."

So, sadly, the curse was over. Chuck Tanner went on to manage the team to a world championship in 1979, keeping the job for nine seasons until a man not named Danny Murtaugh (it was actually Jim Leyland) replaced him. While we talk about a curse in this chapter, make no mistake, Danny Murtaugh is a beloved figure in Pirate lore—and a hell of a manager, finishing with an 1115–950 record, four division titles and two world championships. It was no wonder Brown kept the curse alive for so many years.

CHAPTER 30

1976: CURTAIN CALL

BACKED INTO A CORNER, THE STEELERS' STEEL CURTAIN HAD A SEASON FOR THE AGES AND BECAME THE SQUAD TO WHICH ALL GREAT DEFENSES ARE COMPARED

By Chris Fletcher

The Steelers were coming off back-to-back Super Bowl wins. The smart money said a third one, something not done since the Green Bay Packers a decade earlier, was inevitable—if they stayed healthy. A big *if,* it turned out. And though they avoided it before, there was a bit of the dreaded Super Bowl hangover.

It started in game one against the rival Oakland Raiders. For three quarters, the Steelers had their way with the Raiders, running out to a 28–14 lead. But the Raiders rallied to tie the score thanks to a blocked punt and more late-game heroics from Oakland quarterback Kenny Stabler. And when quarterback Terry Bradshaw pressed the issue with an ill-timed interception, the final read Oakland 31, Pittsburgh 28.

The Steel Curtain had blown a big lead. But the game had a more lasting effect on both teams. For the Raiders, the win brought confidence against the team that had eliminated them three out of the four past years. For the Steelers, letting it slip away led to a funk.

It continued the next week against the Browns, with the Steelers fortunate to rally from a 14–0 deficit for a 31–14 win. Bradshaw was ineffective, completing only 7 of 23 passes for 77 yards. Game three against the Patriots was more of the same. Six turnovers in the first half led to a 30–27 loss as kicker Roy Gerela's game-tying field goal attempt fell short as time expired.

When the 1976 Pittsburgh Steelers stood at 1–4 and Terry Bradshaw was lost to the team with an injury, many thought a disastrous season was on the horizon as Chuck Noll turned to rookie quarterback Mike Kruczek out of Boston College. The Steeler demise never happened, as the rookie led them to six consecutive wins before Bradshaw returned. While he played well, it's worth noting that he had a tremendous running game and one of the greatest defenses in league history to help him engineer those wins. *Photo courtesy of Boston College Athletics.*

The free fall continued against the Vikings. Despite a stout defensive effort, the Steelers couldn't overcome six turnovers in a 17–6 loss. And then came the low point in the rematch against the Browns.

In the rematch, the Steelers lost more than the game. They also lost Bradshaw when the Browns' Joe "Turkey" Jones brutally dumped the quarterback onto the turf helmet first. Sitting at 1–4 with their starting quarterback out and the offense shaky at best, it was time for the defense to take over if the Steelers were to have even a slim chance of making the playoffs, let alone even thinking of a three-peat.

The Steelers had built their championships on the strength of the Steel Curtain—a mix of physical and cerebral superstars. It started with physical domination of Mean Joe Greene, the anchor of the line and arguably the greatest player in franchise history even to this day. Greene redefined the defensive tackle position and forced opponents to double and even triple team him, opening up opportunities for the fellow members of the front four.

On one end was the speedy L.C. Greenwood, who retired as the franchise's all-time leader in sacks. Next, and nearly as unstoppable physically as Greene, was Ernie "Fats" Holmes. Surprisingly, he never appeared in a Pro Bowl game, but he was disruptive and may have been the strongest man on the team. Rounding out the front four was Dwight White, the Super Bowl hero only two years before, who got out of a hospital bed to play. But 1976 was challenging for White, who battled injuries all year. His place was taken admirably by John Banaszak. The line's mission was to clog the line of scrimmage so that the team's cadre of linebackers could make plays.

And what a linebacking core it was—sporting two Hall of Famers and another player who should be inducted. In the middle, Jack Lambert combined physicality with intimidation. He had his best season, capturing NFL Defensive Player of the Year honors. On the outside was another Hall of Famer. Jack Ham, a graduate of Penn State's "Linebacker U," was a master of technique. He was as skilled covering a back or tight end as he was stuffing the run or rushing the quarterback. The final linebacking position was shared by Andy Russell, a six-time Pro Bowler, who should be in Canton, and newcomer Loren Toews, a speedy defender and eager learner. For Russell, it was the final year of a storied career that dated back to the '60s and its moribund Steelers teams.

The defensive backfield was loaded, too. Corner Mel Blount, another Hall of Famer, played a physical brand of football, jamming receivers at the line to effectively shut them down. Blount was so dominant that the NFL changed the rules to make it illegal to contact receivers five yards from the line of scrimmage. The other corner, J.T. Thomas, was a ferocious hitter who could stuff the run as well as cover. He also had a knack for the big play—as did safety Glen Edwards, who had created turnovers in the past two Super Bowls. The other safety, Mike Wagner, was the quarterback of the defense, responsible for calling coverages. The starters were so good that Donnie Shell, a future Hall of Famer, was a part-time player.

Stepping in for Bradshaw was rookie Mike Kruczek. He had a clear directive: don't do anything stupid, hand the ball off to running backs Franco Harris and Rocky Bleier and get out of the way. The team's slim path to the playoffs was to be paved by a grinding running game and a stout defense.

Yet no one could have expected just how stout the Steel Curtain would be. It started with a key divisional matchup against the Bengals. The defense dominated, shutting down Pro Bowl quarterback Ken Anderson, sacking him five times and intercepting him twice in a 23–6 win. The D was even sharper the following week against the Giants, allowing only 151 yards while shutting out the G-Men, 27–0. The defense made it back-to-back shutouts, crushing the San Diego Chargers 23–0. The Steelers allowed only seven first downs and 134 net yards. The next week brought Bradshaw's return, not that it mattered. The Steelers posted a third straight shutout as they crushed Kansas City 45–0.

The Dolphins ended the scoreless streak, but they could only muster a field goal. The Steelers won 14–3 but lost Bradshaw to injury again. Kruczek was again under center for a crucial divisional game against the Oilers. Houston was the first team in 22 quarters to find the Steelers' end zone, but it wasn't nearly enough. The Steel Curtain battered quarterback John Hadl and intercepted him twice.

That set the stage for the rematch with the division-leading Bengals. By now, the Steelers knew every game mattered, but this one would all but determine their playoff fate. In a driving snowstorm, the Steelers' ground game was the difference. Though they only put up one touchdown, it was enough, as the Bengals were limited to a field goal, with Pittsburgh winning 7–3.

The Steelers closed out the season with consecutive shutouts against two cupcake teams, crushing Tampa Bay 42–0 and Houston 21–0. It also closed out the most remarkable defensive stand in league history. In nine games, the D allowed only 28 points. Even more incredibly, they surrendered only one touchdown.

Thanks to the Steel Curtain, the team finished 10–4 and took the AFC Central crown and a fifth straight playoff appearance. Heading into the playoffs, the team was brimming with confidence. Outscoring your opponents 234–28 will do that. Not surprisingly, they blew out the Colts 40–14. Once again, the defense was brilliant, stifling quarterback Bert Jones.

But the victory was costly. Both Harris and Bleier were injured. Surprisingly, coach Chuck Noll opted to keep Franco in the game despite the huge lead. They would have to play the AFC Championship Game against the Raiders without a bona fide back.

The game was like a flashback to the opener. Oakland ran up a 10–0 lead thanks to an interception and a partially blocked punt. Although the Steelers scored on a short run, Oakland closed out the half with a momentum-changing touchdown, when Raider quarterback Stabler hit former Steeler Warren Bankston on a four-yard touchdown pass with only 19 seconds left in the half. Then the Raiders took control by taking away the Steelers' running game and forcing Bradshaw and the offense to pass. He finished 14 of 35 and couldn't find the end zone again. The final: Oakland 24, Pittsburgh 7.

In a 1995 interview, owner Dan Rooney reflected on the '76 defense and its remarkable season. "It may have been our most dominant team," he recalled. "But in the end, we didn't win it all. Still, give me that defense and I like our chances against anybody." For a team that defined winning in the 1970s, it's ironic that its best squad was the one that came up short. But it's still one deserving of a curtain call.

CHAPTER 31

1976: A HOMETOWN TRAGEDY

By Frank Garland

His 1976 season behind him, Bob Moose wasn't sure where he would find himself pitching the next spring.

Or if he would be pitching anywhere at all, for that matter.

The Export, Pennsylvania native, whose mercurial stint with the Pittsburgh Pirates included such gems as a no-hitter as well as maddening stretches of inconsistency and a famous wild pitch that ended the Pirates' bid at repeating as World Champions in 1972, finished the '76 campaign on a down note. In fact, speculation was that he might have thrown his final pitch for his hometown club.

"Moose was an excellent pitcher just a few months ago," wrote Bob Smizik in the October 4 edition of the *Pittsburgh Press*. "But he slipped so badly after July that the Pirates may try to send him elsewhere. There are sure to be teams that will give him a try."

Indeed, the numbers did not paint a rosy picture for the stocky right-hander. In his final 10 appearances, which included one start and nine relief outings, Moose surrendered 31 hits and 17 earned runs in 21⅓ innings for a 7.17 ERA, walking 10 and striking out 11.

But Moose's baseball future—and his life—were cut short less than a week later.

The Monroeville resident, who was celebrating his 29th birthday at a golf outing/dinner party near Martins Ferry, Ohio, on October 9, died when he lost control of his car in the rain on Ohio Route 7 and collided head-on with a second vehicle driven by 17-year-old Stephen George of Yorkville, Ohio.

Shown swinging and missing is Export, Pennsylvania native Bob Moose (No. 38). Moose had a fine career with his hometown team before he was tragically killed in a car accident on October 9, 1976. *Photo courtesy of the Pittsburgh Pirates.*

Moose had traveled to the area to take part in an annual golf tournament held at a course owned by former Pirate teammate and franchise legend Bill Mazeroski. According to news reports, Moose stopped at a restaurant, went to his hotel to change clothes and was returning to the restaurant, where he was to meet several past and present teammates for dinner, when the accident occurred at approximately 9:35 p.m.

News of Moose's death hit the Pirate family hard.

"Here's a young man in the prime of his life, alive and healthy one minute and not with us anymore the next," said Moose's former manager Danny Murtaugh, who resigned as skipper just the week before the accident. "I can't tell you how depressing that is."

Pirates general manager Joe Brown called Moose's death a tragedy, particularly for Moose's wife, Alberta, and their five-year-old daughter, April. "There are a lot of fine ballplayers but Bob was a very special kind of person," Brown said. "He overcame an injury that almost ended his career. It's very shocking to lose someone so vibrant and full of life."

Moose's Pirates teammates stepped up after the fatal accident; several of them, including Al Oliver, helped create the Bob Moose Memorial Fund to benefit young April Moose.

"We want April to learn that her father was somebody special," Oliver said at a press conference announcing the fund's formation.

Tributes poured in from around the baseball world. Pete Rose, then with the Cincinnati Reds, said, "Bob Moose was my kind of player. He would fight you down to the bitter end."

Moose nearly lost his life in late May 1974 when a blood clot that caused his right arm to swell to nearly twice its normal size sent him to the hospital for emergency surgery. Along with having the clot removed, Moose had to have a rib removed, and that initial surgery was followed by a second procedure to remove a hematoma.

"That first operation wasn't bad," Moose told Pat Livingston, sports editor of the *Pittsburgh Press*, "but that second one, five days later, was something else. I didn't know if I was going to make it. For four or five days I didn't know where I was. I didn't even know I was in a hospital."

The blood clot came upon Moose suddenly. He was warming up in the bullpen on the night of May 29, and his arm started swelling. He went immediately to the trainer's room in the Pirates' clubhouse. "The arm was all blue…the whole arm…and it was swollen to twice its size," Pirates trainer Tony Bartirome told a reporter the next day.

Dr. Joseph Finegold, the Pirates' team physician, described the initial surgery as "very difficult, very serious."

As it turned out, Moose missed the rest of the '74 campaign. But the bulldog-like hurler, considered by many to be the best athlete ever to play at what was then Franklin Area High School, was determined to regain his spot on the Pirates roster in 1975, and he did so.

He originally staked a claim to that spot as a raw 19-year-old after just parts of three seasons in Pittsburgh's minor league system. He made his big-league debut at the age of 19 on September 19 at the Houston Astrodome, where he started and worked 5⅔ innings, giving up seven hits and five earned runs. He rebounded from that rocky start by pitching a complete-game seven-hitter in a 4–1 win over the same Houston club on a frigid night at Forbes Field. Moose walked just two and struck out five in going the distance before just 2,269 fans—at least 50 of whom were his friends and family members.

Moose would have more memorable moments. In his first full season in 1968—the so-called year of the pitcher—Moose went just 8–12 but fashioned a 2.74 ERA and an outstanding 1.037 WHIP. He followed that up with a sizzling 14–3 mark and a 2.91 ERA in 1969, the year that included his no-hit effort over a New York Mets team that would go on to win the World Series.

He had several more solid campaigns in the coming years; he went 11–7 for the Pirates' World Series championship team in 1971 and followed that up with a 13–10 mark and a 2.91 ERA in the ill-fated 1972 season. But in his final two seasons following his blood clot surgery, he went a combined 5–11 with a 3.72 ERA.

Overall for his career, Moose was 76–71 with a 3.50 ERA in 289 games, 160 of which were starts. In 1,303⅓ innings, Moose yielded 1,308 hits, struck out 827 and walked 387.

For all of his accomplishments, Moose is likely best remembered for delivering a ninth-inning wild pitch that decided the 1972 National League Championship Series in favor of the Cincinnati Reds. Moose came on in relief of Dave Giusti, who had given up a game-tying home run to Johnny Bench leading off the ninth and then allowed the next two hitters to reach safely.

Moose nearly got out of the inning unscathed, getting the first two batters he faced. But his wild pitch to Hal McRae sent George Foster scurrying home with the game-winning—and series-winning—run, ending the Pirates' bid for back-to-back World Series championships.

Still, that's not what Oliver remembers when someone mentions Bob Moose. Instead, in a 2022 interview, Oliver remembered an incident in Atlanta 51 years earlier when the Braves' Ron Herbel "had the audacity" to hit Oliver with a pitch. "Moose was the type of guy who always protected his hitters," Oliver recalled. "I went out to center field, and Ralph Garr came to the plate. Moose threw a pitch, Ralph hit the deck and Ralph's helmet flew off. And from what I saw, it looked like the ball went between Ralph's helmet and his head.

"As a teammate, that did not surprise me. That's the way Bob was. He protected his players, and that's the one thing I always remembered about Bob Moose. He was a good man."

CHAPTER 32

1976: PERFECTION

PITT IS CROWNED NATIONAL CHAMPIONS

By David Finoli

P erfection! It's the lofty goal of every college football team, although one that is rarely achieved. When the University of Pittsburgh hired coach Johnny Majors to take over arguably the worst major college football program in the land before the 1973 campaign, perfection either then or four years later wasn't even in the back of their mind. In 1975, when the team stood a disappointing 6–3 heading into their final two games of the year against nationally ranked Notre Dame and Penn State, two programs they hadn't beaten in a very long time, a 6–5 campaign was a very real possibility. That would have stuck the program in neutral, making virtually no progress in Majors' third season. Luckily, they not only upset the Irish 34–20 on a day when Tony Dorsett ran for a then-school-record 303 yards but also outplayed the Nittany Lions in a 7–6 loss and then received a bowl bid where they crushed Kansas in the Sun Bowl 33–19. All of a sudden, they were being mentioned in the short list of national championship contenders for 1976, and the thought of perfection didn't seem so ludicrous after all.

While those final three games of the 1975 campaign seemed to give this team the confidence they needed to take the program to the next level, they would begin 1976 in a challenging fashion as ABC wanted a high-profile matchup to start the season. The first national broadcast would be Pitt traveling to South Bend to play their rivals from Notre Dame, and the Irish, very angry from the beating they took at Pitt Stadium the year before, were looking for revenge on their home turf.

Playing for the New England Patriots was Pitt quarterback Matt Cavanaugh (No. 12). After starting quarterback Robert Haygood was lost for the season against Georgia Tech in 1976, Cavanaugh came to the rescue and gave the Pitt offense something it didn't have before: a passing element. He helped lead the team to the national championship that season. *Photo courtesy of University of Pittsburgh Athletics.*

It had been quite a ride over the previous three seasons after the Panthers brought Majors aboard. He immediately took the club from an embarrassing state to a bowl team in his first year. For years, they had been limited to 25 recruits as part of the Big Four agreement with Penn State, Syracuse, West Virginia and themselves, and in 1974, the NCAA would limit all programs to only 30 recruits, so they had to take advantage of the 1973 class, from which they could sign an unlimited number of players. In a 2006 *Tribune-Review* article, then defensive coordinator Jackie Sherill, who eventually took over after Majors left for Tennessee in 1977, recalled he believed they signed 76 players. He remembered Majors told them to "bring in anybody who can help us win. We just put our heads down and our rear ends up and started digging." What they brought in was the likes of Cecil Johnson, Ed Wilamowski, Al Romano, Arnie Weatherington, Robert Haygood, Don Parrish, John Pelusi, Jim Corbett and a speedy running back from Hopewell High School who became the school's only Heisman Trophy winner to date,

Tony Dorsett. All were pivotal members of the 1976 squad. Still, beating Notre Dame at South Bend would be a difficult battle.

The groundskeeper made sure the grass was long in an effort to help slow down Dorsett, and it looked even more troubling when the Irish took the ball on an 86-yard drive to open the game with a touchdown and a 7–0 lead. When Pitt got the ball back, they immediately put it in Dorsett's hands, and he rambled 61 yards to set up Pitt's first touchdown. Apparently, not even long grass could slow him down. What the sellout crowd of 59,035 didn't know was that the game was all but over at that time. Pitt scored 31 of the next 34 points to win in an impressive manner 31–10 as Tony D. finished with 181 yards. If they had lacked any confidence they could be a national championship contender at the beginning of the season, they sure didn't now.

While they crushed Georgia Tech the next week 42–14, they would have to see how good their depth was at quarterback when they lost starter Robert Haygood for the season with a knee injury. Majors knew there would be no dropoff at quarterback as backup Matt Cavanaugh came in. Haygood certainly was a superior runner and did an outstanding job with the option, but Cavanaugh gave the team another element that would prove to be dangerous: an arm. Teams now had to defend against the pass, something he showed against Duke in week four.

Following a 21–7 win over Temple, a game that Pitt trailed 7–6 at the half, they crushed the Blue Devils 44–31 as Cavanaugh threw for 339 on 17 attempts. A once-dangerous offense was now almost impossible to stop. The next week, with Pitt up 27–0 at the half and Dorsett passing Ed Marinaro for second on the all-time NCAA rushing list, Cavanaugh suffered a hairline fracture at the top of his left ankle. It wasn't season ending, but he would miss at least a couple games. Majors was now in trouble. He'd go to third-string quarterback Tom Yewcic, who had no game experience to this point. No problem, though. He had Tony Dorsett to hand the ball off to.

In a 36–19 win over Miami (Florida), he rambled for 227 yards. The next week, at Navy, a team who upset the Panthers 17–0 in 1975, he continued his onslaught against the record books. With only four yards needed to break Archie Griffin's all-time NCAA rushing mark, he broke loose on a 32-yard touchdown run to do it in style as Pitt got their revenge over the Midshipmen 45–0 to move to 7–0.

With perfection in sight, they ran into a sophomore quarterback by the name of Bill Hurley who led Syracuse to a 13–10 lead in the third quarter, which threatened the Panthers' perfect mark. Tony had a goal of becoming the first back in collegiate history to amass 6,000 yards and added to his total with 241 against the Orangemen as the Panthers scored the game's final 13 points in a 23–13 win an avert the upset.

There was nothing special about the Panthers' ninth consecutive victory, a 37–7 win against Army at Pitt Stadium, although it was special in the sense that Cavanaugh made his return—and oh yeah, top-ranked Michigan lost to Purdue 16–14, which put second-ranked Pitt as the number one team in the land. When they announced the score at the stadium, the 45,573 fans were ecstatic. It was a position Pitt held on to the next week at home, with a 24–16 win in the backyard brawl setting up a regular season–ending contest against Penn State at Three Rivers Stadium.

Pitt had never beaten Joe Paterno to this point and hadn't beaten a Nittany Lions squad since 1965. When Penn State went up 7–0 early on and were very successful in holding Dorsett at bay, many in the sold-out stadium had to wonder if perfection was coming to an end. The Panthers tied it going into the half but were struggling as they had rarely done this season. In the locker room, Majors decided to go to an unbalanced line and run Dorsett from fullback in the I formation rather than the split back veer. The results were dramatic. Tony ran for 224 yards, eclipsing 6,000 for his career, and the Panthers ended their Nittany Lion losing streak by scoring the game's final 17 points in a 24–7 victory.

They now needed only one more win to cap the perfect season and a national championship, but they had to beat fifth-ranked Georgia in the Sugar Bowl. Majors let his team enjoy New Orleans early in the week while Bulldog coach Vince Dooley kept his players under curfew. Georgia fans were abusing the Panther players in the city, and by the end of the week, as the game approached, Pitt just wanted to show the fans and the Georgia players just how superior they were. Game MVP Matt Cavanaugh threw for 191 yards and Dorsett rambled for 202 as the Panthers built a 21–0 halftime lead on their way to a dominant 27–3 victory.

The amazing turnaround was complete, and perfection was achieved. Even the news that Majors was returning to his alma mater, Tennessee, to coach the following year couldn't put a damper on what Pitt accomplished. After all, perfection is a goal that all want and precious few achieve. The 1976 Pitt Panthers did.

CHAPTER 33

1977: THE TRADITION

WESTMINSTER WINS BACK-TO-BACK NATIONAL TITLES

By David Finoli

While Pitt winning the National Championship came as a surprise for many Western Pennsylvania football fans, especially considering the state of the program in 1972, when Westminster College in New Wilmington, Pennsylvania, right outside New Castle, defeated Cal Lutheran 17–9 in a thrilling comeback victory to win the 1977 NAIA Division II Football Championship, it came as surprise to no one. After all, they were champions in 1976 and had a 21–1 mark over two seasons that included 20 wins in a row. The win gave the school three national championships in its history, a number that increased by three a decade and a half later when they won back-to-back again in 1988 and 1989 before capturing their last one to date in 1994.

After the team defeated Anderson College at Taggart Stadium in New Castle 21–16 to capture their first title in 1970 under longtime coach Hall of Famer Harold Burry, he turned the reins over to Joe Fusco two years later, in 1972. Fusco was an offensive guard for Burry between 1957 and 1959. Following his graduation from Westminster in 1960, he wanted to become as accomplished a head coach as Burry had been, taking the head coach spot at Wilmington Area High School that same year. He stayed there until 1966, when he moved over to Grove City Area High as the head man for one season. In 1968, he came back to his alma mater as an assistant to Burry until he finally replaced the Hall of Famer, hoping to keep the tradition alive.

Fusco's first few teams were very successful, going 27–5–1, but they had fallen short of the school's yearly goal, being selected to the NAIA Division II playoffs. That frustrating streak would end a year later, in 1976. They began the season with a 20–7 victory over Susquehanna before a disappointing 14–7 loss to Juniata. It would be the last time they'd be disappointed for nearly two years. Starting with a 6–2 victory over Indiana University of Pennsylvania (IUP), they reeled off eight consecutive wins following a semifinal upset over top-ranked Texas Lutheran 31–0 to secure a spot in the national championship game against Redlands College. In the eight games, their stingy defense had allowed only 32 points, while their offense scored 210. On the road in Redlands, California, the two teams battled and were tied at 13 going into the final quarter when Titans quarterback Jan Budai ran it in from three yards out for the game's final points in a 20–13 victory. With their second national championship in hand, Westminster was now a confident team and wanted to make sure the rest of the nation knew it.

It was a team that had a solid defense and offensive line led by four first team All-Americans. Linebacker Frank Emanuele and defensive tackle Mark Claire both would be named first team All-Americans on two occasions, with Emanuele given the honor in 1976 and 1977 and Claire being named in 1977 and 1978. On the offensive, line guard Mark Humphrey was on the first team the same two seasons as Emanuele while offensive tackle Paul O'Neil was on the '77 squad. The group was joined by two academic All-Americans in offensive tackle, Paul Rice and linebacker Scott McLuckey.

After defeating their first three opponents by relatively easy scores, they took on their toughest team of the season to that point, Waynesburg College. Ranked number one in the nation with a 12-game winning streak, Westminster crushed Waynesburg in 1976 33–7, but this game would not be easy. Starting quarterback Steve Kraus threw for 152 yards for the game, including a 17-yard toss to Regis Coyne, to give the Titans a comfortable 17–3 lead at the half. In the fourth quarter, after stopping Westminster at the one-yard line, which would have turned this game into a rout, the Yellow Jackets went on a 99-yard drive but missed the extra point to bring Waynesburg to within eight points. Running back Bob Albert then scored late to make the score 17–15 but missed on the two-point conversion as the Titans held on to extend their winning streak to 13. It was as close to a loss as they'd come in the regular season, allowing only 13 points in their final five contests to head into the playoffs with the streak now at 18.

They were awarded the Lambert Trophy as the best small college team in the East not long after defeating West Virginia's Concord College in a thrilling semifinal contest. On a rainy day in New Wilmington, it was a matchup against the top two defensive teams in Division II of the NAIA. After tying the score at six when the Titans' Steve Nelson picked off a pass from Concord quarterback Jeff Boyles and took it 43 yards for the touchdown, Boyles got revenge with a 16-yard scoring toss to Tony Lipscomb, putting the visitors up 13–6 with 9:11 left in the contest after recovering a Westminster fumble at the 24.

Going up against such a tough defense, which had stopped their offense all day, Fusco and his team showed what championship character was. The Titans took the ball downfield, with Kraus hitting tight end John Wilkie in the corner of the end zone to bring them to within a point at 13–12 with only 5:05 left. It was cold, and it was raining still, and after each team missed an extra point—as well as the fact that his kicker Walt Sieminski had a knee injury—Fusco didn't want to put his kicking team out there, so he went for the lead. Kraus found Dave Hasson for the two-point conversion, and the defense held on to give Westminster a trip to the final. Fusco was thrilled after the victory, saying in a *Pittsburgh Post-Gazette* article, "We didn't panic or worry about being behind. The game goes so fast, we didn't even think about being behind." He went on to say that "there's no pressure here at all. The only pressure is the pressure of tradition. We don't have alumni telling us we have to win." But they had the pressure of the tradition of winning, which would be on display the next week as they traveled to Thousand Oaks, California, to take on Cal Lutheran in the national championship game.

The last time the Titans traveled to Thousand Oaks was in 1971, when they lost to their opponents 30–14, and it looked like they'd fare no better in this contest. They were an injured team, with their leading rusher, Coyne, and Mike DeChellis not available for the game as they fell behind 9–0 in the third quarter. The situation worsened: Kraus was gone with a shoulder injury and had to be replaced by Ray Lyerly. At this point, down nine with three starters gone on offense, the prospects for extending their 19-game winning streak looked bleak. Most schools might have given up, but most teams didn't have to live up to the tradition that Westminster did. Backup running back Frank Rondinelli decided to show off first his arm, then his legs. The Sewickley native first hit Bill Stiger with a 48-yard touchdown pass to cut the lead to two. Then, following a 19-yard fourth-quarter field goal by Sieminski, which gave the visitors their first lead of the day, Rondinelli, the game's offensive MVP, ran 36 yards for the game-clinching score and a 17–9 lead. The Titan defense was now inspired and held on, led by Pittsburgh Central Catholic alum Emanuele, the defensive MVP after picking off a pass and recovering a fumble. It gave Westminster their 20th consecutive victory and added to the tradition with a third national championship.

Eventually, Fusco led them once again to back-to-back titles in 1988 and 1989, this time with a 27-game winning streak, and like his predecessor, he was elected to the College Football Hall of Fame in 2001 with a 154–34–3 mark. He did what is tough to do: follow a legend and keep the tradition alive, something that was very apparent on this day in California in 1977.

CHAPTER 34

1977: THE DAY THAT LIVES IN INFAMY

DUQUESNE'S LAST NCAA MEN'S BASKETBALL APPEARANCE

By David Finoli

The 1970s were not kind to Duquesne basketball, so there's only one slot in this book devoted to the team. I know it probably should have been 1971, the year they went 21–4 and finished the season ranked 15th in the country, but they lost in the first round of the NCAA Tournament, which made it a disappointing year. I almost went with the 1979 team that began the last era of truly winning basketball at the school, but despite capturing two Eastern Eight regular season titles, they never made the NCAA tourney and probably had their best year in 1980–81—not good for a book on the 1970s. No, we decided to go with this 1977 season, a year they finished under .500 in the regular season before, stunningly, capturing the first Eastern Eight (eventually becoming the Atlantic 10) tournament, thus securing themselves a spot in the NCAA tourney. Important? Probably not. But it has become a rallying point for all Duquesne alums and fans of the team. It's the day we all look at as our day of continual suffering for what might be eternity, a day that lives in infamy for us: the last time a Duquesne men's basketball team has ever made an NCAA Men's Basketball Tournament.

For a time near the middle of the 20th century, Duquesne University men's basketball were the Kings on the Bluff. The program was among the best in the nation, constantly competing for a national championship, something the team finally achieved in 1955 when Dick Ricketts and Sihugo Green led them to a victory over Dayton for the National Invitation

One of the greatest players ever to wear a Duquesne Dukes uniform, Norm Nixon (No. 10) led the team to the Eastern Eight Tournament title in 1977 and a berth in the NCAA tournament. To date, it is the last time the school has ever received a bid to the tourney. *Photo courtesy of Duquesne University Athletics.*

Tournament championship, back when the NIT was as important as the NCAA tournament, if not more so. While their place among the nation's elite began to slip as they went into the 1960s, Red Manning, who replaced the wildly successful Dudey Moore as head coach of the Dukes, seemed to be leading them back to national prominence with a Sweet Sixteen appearance in 1969 where they finished ninth in the final Associated Press poll. Two years later, they made the tournament again, losing to Penn in the first round of the tourney. By 1973–74, the team had slipped to .500 at 12–12 as Manning retired from the bench to concentrate on the athletic director job at the school.

John Cinicola took over at that point and could muster up only a 26–24 record in his first two seasons. Things continued to fall in his third season as the program entered conference play for the first time. They had entered the Eastern Collegiate Basketball League, more commonly referred to as the Eastern Eight, a league that eventually turned into their current affiliation, the Atlantic 10. It was a collection of some of the finest schools in the region: Rutgers, Villanova, George Washington, UMass, West Virginia, Penn State, Pitt and the Dukes, of course. Duquesne didn't fare well that first season with a 4–7 record in the Western Division, finishing the regular season overall at 12–14. They went into that first conference tournament with not much hope, going up against Penn State in the first round at the Spectrum in Philadelphia.

Duquesne found their game against the Nittany Lions with a 65–55 upset win and got a break when fourth-seeded UMass upset the top-seeded Rutgers Scarlet Knights 78–74 and would face the Dukes in the semifinals. The Minutemen had finished the season with a 19–10 mark, and even though Cinicola would rather have faced them than the top seed, they would still go into this contest as a decided underdog. It didn't matter, as Duquesne was now playing their best basketball of the season and crushed their favored opponent 82–65 to advance to the first Eastern Eight championship game. There, they faced the hometown Villanova Wildcats, who were led by their well-known and respected coach, Rollie Massimino. Villanova was 20–8 with a signature victory over eighth-ranked Notre Dame.

It was a much tighter game than the last two, but somehow, the underdog role fit this Dukes squad. Norm Nixon was the star of this team, but a 6'5" senior forward by the name of Don Maser would come through in the clutch late in the ballgame. Up by one point, Maser was fouled and needed to hit both shots to clinch the title for Duquesne. It had been only two years before that doctors diagnosed him with a kidney ailment, telling him he'd never play basketball again. Now he was at the line, where he calmly hit both free throws to give the Dukes a 57–54 lead and the conference championship— and with it a trip to the 1977 NCAA tournament against the Virginia Military Institute.

The date was March 12, 1977, and the hope was that they could continue the momentum from their stunning tournament victory. Nixon had a terrific contest with 27 points, while Maser continued his fine play with 14. They led late in the first half 33–27, and it seemed like their journey would continue. At that point, the glass slipper this Cinderella had been wearing seemed to break. They gave up the final six points of the half with two horrible turnovers as the Keydets tied the contest 33–33. VMI's Dave Montgomery had scored 12 second-half points as VMI continued to increase the lead to 56–49 with 10 minutes left in the regulation. Duquesne had a little bit left in the tank, cutting the advantage to 61–60 at the 4:30 mark, but the Dukes were in foul trouble for most of the game, losing three starters, including Nixon, as the Keydets hit eight foul shots down the stretch for the 73–66 victory.

Cinicola was irritated with the play of his team. In a *Pittsburgh Press* article, he said, "Foul trouble really hurt us and made us change our game, but we were the ones who got ourselves into trouble. We made some dumb fouls." An upset Nixon turned toward his disappointed coach at the end and told him, "That's all right coach, it was fun while it lasted."

He was right, it was fun, but this game is not remembered for the fact that they won an unexpected 1977 Eastern Eight championship and made the tourney. It's remembered more for the beginning of 40-plus years of torture, 40-plus years of having other fan bases feel sorry for you. It's remembered as the day Duquesne University basketball died (even though there would still be a couple of successful seasons a few years later before the new administration in the early 1980s effectively killed it with some poor decisions).

Today, this game binds alumni and fans alike, who look toward each other for support while hoping one day they will all be able to see their program in the NCAA tournament once again. A time when the suffering will finally come to an end and we can remember their last trip in 1977 more fondly. A day when March 12, 1977, will no longer be remembered as the day that would live in infamy.

CHAPTER 35

1978: SLAYING GOLIATH

JOHN MAHAFFEY COMES BACK TO DEFEAT TOM WATSON AT THE PGA

By David Finoli

Tom Watson and local legend Arnie Palmer had a few things in common over their Hall of Fame golf careers. First off, they became two iconic figures in the sport, remembered as two of the best ever to swing a club. Second was the fact that they both won three legs of the career grand slam, missing only the PGA Championship to complete the rare achievement. For Watson, his best chance came in 1978, when the PGA Championship made a rare appearance in the Steel City, at the famed Oakmont course. After three rounds, he held a five-stroke lead over Jerry Pate and seven strokes over John Mahaffey. Mahaffey went on to shoot a fabulous 66 in the final round as Watson had one of the worst days in his legendary career, forcing a three-man sudden death playoff with Pate. When Mahaffey birdied the second hole with a 12-foot putt, while Watson and Pate could not match it, it ended one of the most epic comebacks in the history of the majors—the greatest comeback, perhaps, if you consider the fact that he was six strokes down with only nine holes left to play in the fourth round—and saddled Watson with a crushing defeat.

In recent years, Oakmont has exclusively held events for the United States Golf Association (USGA), hosting only U.S. Men's and Women's Opens and U.S. Amateurs, but in 1978, it was the home of the PGA Championship for the third time, the first in the current stroke play format, as the other two times, 1922 and 1951, were competed in match play. In 1978, it was a 6,989-

yard, par 71 course designed by Henry Fownes in 1904. It featured the famed "Church Pew" bunkers on the third and fourth holes. The massive sand trap measured 100 by 40 yards. It also had punishing, lightning-fast greens that the members liked to cut twice before rounds when hosting a major tournament. During this event, a consistent rain during the week tamed the legendary course and allowed Watson to become its master.

In the first couple rounds, the local fans were rooting for their hero, 48-year-old legend Arnie Palmer, and local pro Jim Simons, who was enjoying a decent season on the tour. Unfortunately, while Tom Watson had a magnificent 67 and 69 to hold a four-stroke lead over Tom Weiskopf, Joe Inman and Ben Crenshaw, Simons missed the cut by one stroke with a seven over 149, while Palmer shot a miserable 74 and 78, which put him at 10 over. Many other top golfers also missed the cut, including Jack Nicklaus, who was a stroke behind Arnie at 153. After the first round, it looked like Mahaffey would join Simons, Palmer and Nicklaus by missing the cut as he shot a disappointing 75 but, surprisingly, rebounded with a 67 in the second round to tie Pate at even par, in sixth place with five other golfers that included Hubert Green and Lee Trevino.

It was a surprise that Mahaffey had come back. He had a series of emotional and physical issues in the years leading up to the tournament that made folks question if he would ever be a successful golfer again. On the physical end, he had a hyperextended elbow in 1976 that was followed by a broken wrist he suffered after falling off a ladder in his workshop a year later. He was never the longest hitter on tour but had a great short game. It all went to hell following his injuries; those coupled with his mental issues dropped him to 150th on the money list in 1977 with $9,847.

Mahaffey went through a difficult divorce as well as losing two majors that he should have been victorious in—painful losses. In 1975, he lost the U.S. Open to Lou Graham in an 18-hole playoff after letting the lead slip away. A year later, in 1976, when Pate won his U.S. Open, Mahaffey had the lead with three holes left and couldn't finish. Pate claimed he couldn't fully enjoy his victory because of the pain Mahaffey went through with the loss, saying he hadn't been the same golfer since. Luckily, Mahaffey had remarried, and his wife was fully supportive of his career. It seemed to all make a difference as he continued to play well into the third round with a 68 that put him at three under, two behind Pate, who shot a 66 on the day. They were still far behind Watson, who once again mastered Oakmont with a 67 and was now 10 under for the tournament, five in front of Pate and seven strokes over his friend Mahaffey, whom he called J.D. (for John Drayton, his first and middle names).

Tom was on a collision course with greatness. He had been the leading money winner in 1977, as well as the PGA Tour Player of the Year, and captured the Vardon Trophy for lowest average score on the tour. They were accomplishments he would repeat in 1978 and 1979 to go along with the three majors he had already captured, the Masters the year before as well as the 1975 and 1977 British Opens. He had suffered a great collapse himself in a major, blowing a third-round lead in the 1974 U.S. Open after he fell apart with a final-round 79, to finish five strokes behind Hale Irwin in fifth place. He was older now and had learned to finish. He was the Goliath of the tour at the time, and blowing a five-stroke lead seemed next to impossible, if not just improbable.

The members of Oakmont were furious their course was being abused, especially after the PGA refused to have the greens cut twice in the earlier rounds. Finally, before the final round, they agreed, and the greens became much faster for the participants, except for Mahaffey, who seemed to relish the challenge. It seemed to be a moot point early on as Watson increased his lead to six after the fifth hole, and while Pate had cut into it after eight, coming within two strokes of the leader, Tom nailed a four wood to within three feet of the ninth for an eagle that put him up to four strokes over Pate and six in front of his friend J.D. It was at that point the miracle comeback began to take place.

The next hole saw Watson hit his drive onto a divot, then put one into the sand. After three-putting the hole, he found himself with a double bogey. Mahaffey, on the other hand, put his second shot to within 45 feet on the mercurial greens with seemingly no shot at a birdie. Incredibly, he nailed the putt, and his six-stroke deficit became only two that quickly. Game on!

Mahaffey then hit a 25-foot birdie at 11 before Pate birdied 13, a hole that Watson bogeyed, and there was now a three-way tie for the lead. Mahaffey went ahead by one after the 14th, but his first bogey in 34 holes, on 16, put him back into a tie with Pate. Tom tied Mahaffey with a birdie at 17, and Pate went ahead by one with an easy birdie at the same hole for a one-stroke lead. On 18, Pate hit his first putt to within four feet of the hole. Not his best effort, but still, it was a putt he would make 99 percent of the time. Hole it and the title was his. Miss it and there would be a three-way playoff. Stunningly, his putt rolled around the lip and shot back out. Pate claimed in a *Pittsburgh Press* article, "I hit a good putt. I hit it dead where I wanted to. I never saw one spin out like that. But that's golf."

The tournament, which, only nine holes before, was a boring, one-sided affair, was now going to a thrilling three-man sudden death playoff: Watson, who shot a 73 to blow what was certain victory; Pate, who had a 68; and Mahaffey, who had seemingly turned his career around in his final three rounds at Oakmont and came in at 66. It was only the second sudden death playoff in the history of the PGA Championship, and after each man parred the first hole, they went to the second, where Pate and Watson were looking at par, while Mahaffey had a 12-foot putt that would give him a birdie and his first major championship. He hit the putt and it looked true, dropping into the hole and sending J.D. into the air as he leapt for joy, saying afterward, "It's been a long road back and there's been a lot of disappointments but this makes up for all of that." It certainly did, as both Watson and Pate were genuinely happy for their friend. It was the day that John Mahaffey brought his career back with this epic comeback at Oakmont, the day he slayed Goliath in a tournament few who were there will ever forget.

CHAPTER 36

1978: THE MATURATION OF TERRY BRADSHAW

PITTSBURGH IS BACK ON THE SUPER BOWL–WINNING TRACK

By David Finoli

There was a time early in his career when Terry Bradshaw was looked at as a potential first-round bust. He would flash his immense talent at times but then would make a poor decision that would put the game in peril. Drafting Franco Harris in 1972 gave the Steelers an effective running game, which helped the offense, but still, Terry wasn't close to the championship-winning quarterback most had envisioned. He lost his job to Joe Gilliam in 1974 before recapturing it at mid-season. He improved and did well enough to help the team to a Super Bowl IX title.

As the years went on, he continued to get better, but the team around him looked like it was slipping, and after a disappointing 1977 campaign, it was thought the championship days were behind this franchise. The solution to fix things: set Terry Bradshaw free. With a rule in place that would keep wide receivers open—ironically, a rule the press named after his teammate Mel Blount as the league was attempting to nullify his aggressive play at corner back, making it illegal to impede the opposing wide receiver's progress once they were five yards downfield—Bradshaw was the quarterback in the league who took full advantage as the Pittsburgh Steeler offense went from three yards and a cloud of dust to an aggressive passing one. The results: Bradshaw became the best quarterback in the league, and the Steelers went from a team on a downward spiral to arguably the best in the history of the game.

For the first half of Terry Bradshaw's NFL career, many considered him a disappointment, having a career that wasn't good enough for a player who was the number one overall pick in the draft. In 1975, he began to improve his game, and in 1978, he became one of if not the best quarterback in the league once Chuck Noll opened up the Steeler offense. *Photo courtesy of Louisiana Tech Athletics.*

It had been a difficult couple years for the franchise after capturing back-to-back Super Bowls in 1974 and 1975. In 1976, Bradshaw was hurt after the Steelers started the season with a poor 1–4 record. Perhaps the greatest defensive effort in the history of the game turned around what could have been a losing season as the team won its final nine contests and crushed the Baltimore Colts in the first round of the playoffs. In that game, unfortunately, Franco Harris and Rocky Bleier, both 1,000-yard backs during the regular season, were injured and unavailable for the AFC championship in Oakland, which the team lost, thus ending their attempt at three consecutive NFL Championships. The next year was even worse for Pittsburgh. They never really got on track, even though they won the Central Division. It was with a mediocre 9–5 record. They didn't win until the final day of the season, when Houston upset Cincinnati to give them a gift they didn't expect. The next week, in the first round of the playoffs, they gave up the final 13 points of the game to Denver in a 34–21 loss. Bradshaw played better than he had in his injury-plagued 1976 campaign, which saw him miss six games. He did play hurt, though, needing a hard cast to protect his fractured left wrist, but he threw for a career-high 2,523 yards. He was named team MVP for his efforts.

Things were looking up for the Shreveport, Louisiana native, but his championship days appeared to be at an end. A frustrated Chuck Noll knew changes needed to be made and traded Ernie Holmes, Jim Clack, Jim Allen, Glen Edwards and Frank Lewis. With the Blount Rule now a reality, he also knew he had two of the game's most dynamic receivers in Lynn Swann and John Stallworth—and a strong-armed southern quarterback who had never really lived up to his promise when he was the first selection in the 1970 NFL draft. That would end here as Bradshaw finally reached his potential and then some.

The Steelers opened up the first 16-game season in NFL history (the league dropped the preseason from six to four games before increasing the regular season by two games in 1978) in Buffalo to play the Bills. Bradshaw was almost perfect this day with a 14 for 19 performance for 217 yards and two touchdowns as the team built a 21–0 lead on their way to a 28–17 victory. It gave the team momentum that saw them win their first seven games of the year, including a thrilling 15–9 overtime victory at home against the hated Browns as tight end Bennie Cunningham caught a 37-yard pass from his Hall of Fame quarterback for the winning score.

Following the perfect start, the team went into a mid-season malaise that threatened their championship hopes. They lost in week eight to their division rivals, the Houston Oilers—arguably the second-best team in the league after the Steelers during the final two years of the 1970s—24–17 at Three Rivers Stadium. The troubling part of that contest was the way Houston dominated the lines both offensively and on defense. They followed that up with a narrow victory against a poor Kansas City squad 27–24 and another against an inferior Saints squad 20–14, then Bradshaw had his worst two-game stretch of the year, throwing for only 125 yards and three interceptions against the Rams in a 10–7 loss at Los Angeles, then defeating the 1–10 Bengals 7–6, a game in which the worst team in the league outplayed Pittsburgh as Terry only threw for 117 yards with four interceptions. For the first time during the season, Bradshaw had no touchdown passes, and Swann was without a reception. While the team was 10–2, they played poorly over the previous five games. Noll and his squad had had enough and made sure San Francisco knew it the next game. They crushed the 49ers

24–7 as Bradshaw rebounded with three touchdown tosses and went on to win their final three games, including a 35–13 victory against Baltimore in a driving snowstorm at Three Rivers.

They entered the postseason with a 14–2 mark, tying the NFL record for most wins in a season. In the first round, they took on the Denver Broncos at home, a team they had beaten 21–17 in the final regular season game at Denver. The game stood close after three quarters, with the Steelers clinging to a 19–10 lead. It was at that point they put the game away in a 24-second span as Stallworth caught a 45-yard touchdown pass; then, after Dennis "Dirt" Winston pounced on a fumble during the kickoff return, Swann snagged a 38-yard scoring toss in a 33–10 win.

The next week, in the AFC Championship, the Oilers and Steelers were treated to a nasty, icy rain that contributed to an NFL postseason record 12 fumbles. As the teams were preparing to go in at the half with Pittsburgh up 14–3, thanks to touchdown runs by Harris and Bleier, the home team once again showed their quick strike capabilities. In the final 52 seconds of the half, Swann caught a 29-yard pass for a touchdown; then, after recovering a fumble, Stallworth caught a touchdown toss from 17 yards out to make it 28–3. Finally, they pounced on another Oiler fumble, and Gerela ended the half with a 37-yard field goal to give them a 31–3 lead, en route to a 34–5 victory and another trip to the Super Bowl after a two-year absence. They would get another shot at the Dallas Cowboys, whom they defeated 21–17 in Super Bowl X.

Before Super Bowl XIII, Cowboy linebacker Thomas "Hollywood" Henderson mocked Bradshaw, claiming he was dumb and couldn't spell cat if you spotted him the *c* and the *t*. It was enough to inspire the Steeler quarterback to perhaps the greatest performance in his career. After losing a fumble, which Dallas took in for a score, giving them a 14–7 lead, Bradshaw took over, completing a then–Super Bowl record 75-yard toss to Stallworth to tie the game, then found Bleier from seven yards out, who made a dramatic leaping catch, giving them a 21–14 halftime lead. After Dallas kicked a field goal, cutting the lead to four, Harris went in the final 22 yards of a drive that was set up by a controversial 33-yard pass interference call. Then Swann caught an 18-yard scoring pass after Winston once again recovered a fumble on a kickoff to push Pittsburgh to a 35–17 fourth-quarter advantage. While Dallas scored twice in the final two and a half minutes to make the game artificially close, 35–31, Pittsburgh captured their third Super Bowl championship in an effort that puts them in the short conversation of the NFL's greatest all-time teams.

For Bradshaw, his maturation was complete. He threw for 318 yards and four touchdowns as he was named the game's MVP. For the season, he crushed his career highs with 2,915 yards and 28 touchdowns, being named as a first team All-Pro for the first time and named NFL MVP by the Associated Press, the Maxwell Club and *Sport Magazine*. It was a complete turnaround and the springboard for his eventual election into the Pro Football Hall of Fame, a season for the ages in the annals of Steelers football.

CHAPTER 37

1978: LERCHED

THE PIRATES COME UP SHORT

By David Finoli

By August 12, 1978, the season for the Pittsburgh Pirates was looking like a disaster. Despite the vast talent the team had, they stood at 51–61 following a 10–1 loss to the Philadelphia Phillies and their starting pitcher Randy Lerch. The loss dropped them to 11½ games behind their cross-state rivals as they were mired in fourth place in the National League East, a division they dominated for the first half of the 1970s. It was so bad that had Danny Murtaugh not sadly passed away two years earlier, general manager Joe L. Brown might have replaced Chuck Tanner with him, as he had every other time a manager failed since Murtaugh first retired in 1964. Luckily, the Pirates started winning and went on a 36–11 run following a doubleheader sweep in the first two games of a four-game series to end the season against Philadelphia. The 11½ deficit was down to 1½, and their path to the division championship was simple: win their final two games against the Phils and then a makeup game against the Reds on Monday. Do that, and what was thought to be an impossible dream only a month and a half earlier would become a reality. The only problem was Randy Lerch wouldn't let that happen. He was about to become a verb, as the Bucs were about to be Lerched.

The night before this contest was an exciting doubleheader in which the Pirates defeated the division-leading Phils in the opener 5–4 when catcher Ed Ott opened the bottom of the ninth with a triple off Ron Reed, then came home with the winning run when center fielder Garry Maddox threw the ball away. In the nightcap, Dave Parker doubled to center in the bottom of the ninth and Hall of Fame lefty Steve Carlton intentionally walked Bill Robinson and Willie Stargell to load the bases in hopes of a force-out of a 1–1 contest. In came reliever Warren Brusstar, who promptly balked in the winning run as the 45,134 fans at Three Rivers Stadium were uncontrollably thrilled. With no room for error, the next game, Lerch took the hill, which prompts the following questions:

Question 1: Who was Randy Lerch? Lerch was a second-year lefty who stood 6'5" but only weighed 175 pounds. His nickname was Blade; as Larry Bowa stated in Lerch's biography on SABR.org, he was "thin as a blade but sharp as a razor." While thin, he had one of the better fastballs of the day and enjoyed an 11-year major league career where he was 60–64, a career that was basically nondescript. He enjoyed his best season in 1978, when he won a career high 11 games, the 11th on this evening.

Question 2: What does the verb "Lerched" mean? It basically means that Randy Lerch would beat this team not only with his arm but also with his newly found powerful bat—and one that was quickly powerless, as he hit only one more homer in his career after this contest. And now for the game.

A disappointing crowd of 28,905 was on hand. With everything this game meant, it was thought more would show up, but nonetheless, those who did were thrilled by the end of the first inning. With Don Robinson on the mound, former Pirate heartthrob Richie Hebner doubled in Maddox to give Philadelphia a 1–0 early lead, an advantage that wouldn't last long. They may have eventually been Lerched, but the Philly lefty was not his sharpest in the bottom of the first. He walked Omar Moreno, then gave up singles to Parker and Robinson to load the bases for Stargell. Coming through when they needed him most, Pops promptly smacked his 28th homer to deep center as the Pirates went up 4–1.

The term "Lerched" was in its glory the next inning when the pitcher equaled Willie's shot, also to center, to cut the lead to two runs. Two innings later, the lead was a mere run as Lerch once again homered, this time to deep right as the score was now 4–3. After putting the Bucs down in order in the bottom of the fifth, Lerch was pulled for Brusstar. He needed some help if he was to win this contest and that came in the top of the sixth inning. With Grant Jackson on the mound for Pittsburgh, the Pirate reliever gave up singles to Bake McBride and Maddox. With two out up came the Bull, Greg Luzinski, who smashed a homer to left, and the Phillies were now up 6–4. Lerch was now up for the win.

In the eighth, Kent Tekulve came in, the reliever who won both games the night before, to try to keep the visitors off the scoreboard. If he only had, the Bucs would have eventually won this contest, but Teke might just have been tired throwing his third game in two days. With the bases loaded, Hebner crushed a double to right, which plated three runs, then was brought home on a sacrifice from Mike Schmidt, and this once-hopeful crowd was looking at the wrong end of a 10–4 score. Pittsburgh didn't give up and scored four times in the bottom of the ninth on a ground out by Moreno and singles by Parker and Robinson. With a man on first and Stargell up in another clutch situation, Willie struck out, then Garner grounded out to shortstop Bowa to end the threat, end the game and end the Pirates' hopes.

They won the final game of the year 5–3, but it was too little, too late as they finished the season 1½ games behind. It was an exciting comeback but one that ended when the Pirates were Lerched in the game where the pitcher became a verb.

CHAPTER 38

1979: WE ARE FAMILY

A CHERISHED MEMORY OF THE WORLD CHAMPION PITTSBURGH PIRATES

By David Finoli

Truth be told, the song "We Are Family" by Sister Sledge was never one of my favorite songs. The lyrics, which at one point say, "We are family, I got all my sisters with me," just never made sense for a Major League Baseball team. I was a freshman at Duquesne University in the fall of 1979 and spent most of my first semester at Three Rivers Stadium watching what was a thrilling pennant race. No, I didn't have my best semester from a grade point average perspective; yes, my dad wasn't pleased with it; but I'd rebound nicely over my remaining years and was having a great experience watching them. While I bristled at the beginning when the song started, truth be told, by the end of September, I was caught up with it, standing and dancing every time it blared over the stadium speakers. Five decades later, that remains my most cherished sports experience. In a season of highlights, the following are the key moments.

At the beginning of the season, I was a senior at Greensburg Central Catholic High School and sports editor of the monthly school newspaper, the *Centralite*. I was the sports editor who loved making bold predictions. The rival Philadelphia Phillies signed Pete Rose in the off-season, and many had them as the heavy favorites to capture their fourth straight NL East crown. I wasn't one of them. In my column The Nose Knows (yes, my nose always stood out proudly from my face), I made the claim that signing Dave Parker to the first $1 million contract in professional sports

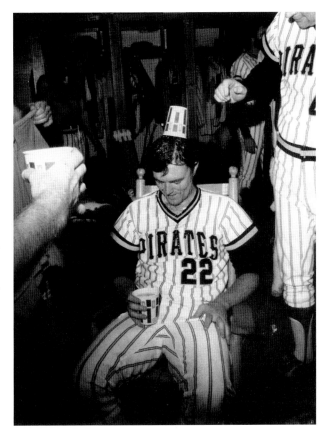

While Bert Blyleven wasn't always happy with the fact that manager Chuck Tanner would pull him from games too often, in game three of the 1979 NLCS, he pitched a fantastic complete game as the Bucs swept the Cincinnati Reds with a dominant 7–1 victory. *Photo courtesy of the Pittsburgh Pirates.*

history was more important than signing Rose, and I made the Bucs the odds-on favorite to win the division. Now, signing Parker was important, but it turned out the following two trades put Pittsburgh over the top. In April, general manager Harding Peterson sent inconsistent shortstop Frank Taveras to the Mets for Tim Foli. Foli gave the team a stable defensive shortstop and also chose 1979 to have his best offensive season with a career high .291 average. In June, Harding gave the Bucs another impressive bat, getting two-time batting champion Bill Madlock (he'd win two more with Pittsburgh) from the Giants for Fred Breining and two of their top young pitchers, Ed Whitson and Al Holland. It was a lot to give up, but it turned the Pirates into champions.

It truly was an exciting pennant race, one where the team battled with the young Montreal Expos instead of the powerful Phillies for control of the division. While the season was full of excitement, four specific contests were the most memorable. The first was August 5 at the stadium against the three-time East champions. It was the first game of a doubleheader, and the Pirates had come back from an 8–3 deficit to tie the game at eight going into the bottom of the ninth. With two outs, Lee Lacy singled, and Rawly Eastwick walked Madlock and Garner to try to set up a force-out. Chuck Tanner brought in lefty pinch hitter John Milner, and the Phils countered with lefty Tug McGraw. Usually, Tanner was a man who like to play the percentages; he decided to leave in Milner for the lefty-on-lefty matchup. Milner promptly smacked the ball over the right field fence for a game-winning grand slam in the 12–8 win.

In late August, the Bucs were in San Diego to face the Padres. I had just gotten to Duquesne, and instead of heading out for a night of fun with my newfound Duquesne friends, I stayed in to watch this matchup. After going down 2–0, Pittsburgh tied it in the ninth to send it onto extra innings. Both teams would score in the 12th as the game went into the wee hours of the morning. As it went on, the guys came back from the bar. First Bob O'Brien, then my roommate Bill Ranier. Gary Degnan, Daryl Dombeck and Sean Christen soon followed. Pretty soon, the lounge was full as newly acquired Dave Roberts loaded the bases against San Diego in the 16th inning with two outs. Pitcher John D'Acquisto came up and Roberts quickly fell behind 3-and-0. Dave Winfield gave Roberts the choke sign at second base, which irritated the hurler. He was now focused and promptly struck out D'Acquisto. He once again loaded the bases in the 17th, this time with no outs, and somehow got out of that crisis giving up no runs. Eventually, the Pirates won in the 19th, and it became a rallying point for the folks I watched the game with. We were all now hooked on the Bucs as this group I was just getting to know became some of my closest friends, most of whom remain friends over 40 years later.

The pennant race was tight, and the two teams were battling as the regular season was coming to an end. After splitting the first two games of an important four-game late-September series against Montreal, the game was tied at three in the bottom of the fifth when the Pirate bats woke up. Pittsburgh scored seven times in the next two innings to cap off a 10–4 victory, putting them up by a half game. Inspired, they crushed the Expos again the next day 10–1 and now had a 1½ game lead with only four left to play. They had to wait until the final day to clinch the division, though. A 5–3 win over the Cubs with 42,176 of us on hand officially gave the team their sixth East Division crown in the 1970s. Their prize, though, was a matchup against the Cincinnati Reds in the NLCS, a team they were 0–3 against in such matchups, losing in 1970, 1972 and 1975.

Being lifted on the arms of his joyous teammates is John Milner. Milner had just hit a pinch-hit grand slam in the bottom of the ninth inning to give Pittsburgh a walk-off 12–8 victory against the Philadelphia Phillies. *Photo courtesy of the Pittsburgh Pirates.*

To break the Reds hex, they had to play the first two games in Cincinnati, and both went to extra innings. In the opening contest, Stargell cracked a three-run homer in the 11th for a 5–2 win. The second game saw Parker single in the winning run in a 3–2 victory that put the Bucs one game away from the National League pennant. Not wanting to leave anything to chance, Pittsburgh scored early and often, while starter Bert Blyleven had his curveball turn nasty. I was there with my Uncle Paul, cousin Fran and brother Jamie. When Blyleven put the finishing touches on a 7–1 win, we were in thorough jubilation. They were going to the World Series, facing the team they beat in 1971, the Baltimore Orioles.

Baltimore won three of the first four games to take a three-to-one lead. The fourth game was the first World Series game I saw in person, and it wasn't a good memory. Baltimore scored six times in the eighth to erase a 6–3 lead, losing 9–6. With supposedly over-the-hill Jim Rooker up next, things looked dire for the Pirates. Years later, at a SABR meeting, Rooker confided to us that the scouts had given the pitchers bad information on the Orioles hitters (back then, few games were on TV, so teams relied very much on scouting reports). He said the Pirate pitchers did the opposite of the scouting reports,

Like Roberto Clemente did in 1971, Willie Stargell took the Pirates on his back in 1979, leading them to their fifth world championship. During the season, he was named MVP for the regular season, NLCS and the World Series. *Photo courtesy of the Pittsburgh Pirates.*

and all of a sudden, Baltimore stopped hitting. The Bucs, surprisingly, won game five 7–1, and then John Candelaria was magnificent in a 4–0 game six victory that tied the series, setting up a seventh and deciding game. While Rich Dauer homered off Jim Bibby in the third to give the Orioles a 1–0 lead, Pops would not be denied, and his two-run homer in the sixth put

Pittsburgh ahead 2–1. We were watching the game at a friend's apartment, a friend who had cable, and Mike Kraut, one of our buddies, was so excited he jumped onto the roof of the building (our friends lived right on the roof, so it wasn't exactly a death-defying leap). Unfortunately, we were kicked out of the building and had to run to the nearest bar to try to see the end of the game. We went into the Carlton House, a ritzy restaurant in Pittsburgh, which let us in despite the fact that we had T-shirts and jeans on. It was there we saw the Pirates score two more runs in the ninth and Omar Moreno grab the final out in a 4–1 victory.

We all took off toward Market Square in the middle of the city to celebrate. It was crammed with excited fans. I looked toward Ranier with a huge smile and said, "I can't wait to do this again next year." Perhaps it jinxed the franchise, as they haven't won another World Series in the five decades since that night. Even though we have yet to celebrate another title run, I cherish the memories of that fabulous season, and I have to admit, I get a big smile on my face every time I hear "We Are Family" on the radio.

CHAPTER 39

1979: CITY OF CHAMPIONS CONFIRMED

STEELERS CAPTURE FOURTH SUPER BOWL

By David Finoli

I t had been quite a run for the city of Pittsburgh between 1978 and 1979. First the Steelers had put on one of the greatest seasons in the history of the National Football League on their way to a 14–2 mark and third Super Bowl championship. Then the Pirates had a memorable, surprising year with the Fam-a-lee climaxing with their fifth World Series championship, coming back from down three games to one to beat the Baltimore Orioles in seven exciting contests. While both became world champions, they did not do so in the same year to validate the claim of City of Champions for the 'Burgh. In 1979, the defense took a bit of a step backward, but the Steeler offense was now one of the best in the game and would confirm what the area already knew: Pittsburgh was truly the City of Champions, as they won back-to-back Super Bowls for the second time.

In 1978, the Steelers made a statement to the rest of the NFL, dominating play on both sides of the ball as they returned to the Super Bowl for the first time in three years. They tied a league record with 14 victories and finished fifth in points scored while leading the league in fewest points allowed on defense. While they'd still be successful a year later, cracks were beginning to show, especially on the defensive side of the ball.

They opened up on a Monday night in Foxboro against a good New England Patriot team and found themselves down 13–6 at the half. The team had lost six players due to injury, including the legendary Joe Greene,

Sitting outside of Acrisure Stadium is a statue of the Chief, Art Rooney. The lovable owner of the Pittsburgh Steelers spent the first 40 years of his ownership generally among the bottom of the standings in the NFL. The 1970s were different, though. By the time the decade was done, he had become the first owner to capture four Super Bowl titles. *Photo courtesy of David Finoli.*

and had to rally late in the fourth quarter when Bradshaw found a wide-open Sidney Thornton in the end zone from 21 yards out to tie the game. Matt Bahr was then successful on a 41-yard field goal in overtime to give the Steelers a 16–13 victory. They crushed Houston in an AFC Championship rematch against the Oilers 38–7 before two extremely close wins against St. Louis and Baltimore put them 4–0 heading to Philadelphia to play the Eagles. Pittsburgh struggled with four turnovers as they played without Lynn Swann in a 17–14 upset loss.

The next week, against the hated Browns in Cleveland, they found their ground game, racking up 361 yards rushing as Franco Harris rambled for 153 yards, including a 71-yard touchdown, and Rocky Bleier had 70 of his 81 yards on an exciting run up the middle for a score in the 51–35 victory. Defensively, they allowed Browns quarterback Brian Sipe to throw for 365 yards as the Steel Curtain defense continued to look nothing like what it had the year before. A crushing 34–7 defeat at the hands of Cincinnati, where they lost seven fumbles, followed before they began to play their best football of the season.

The Steelers crushed the Broncos 42–7 at Three Rivers Stadium and then defeated the Cowboys 14–3 in a matchup that was dubbed Super Bowl XIII$\frac{1}{2}$. There were then dominant wins against Washington and Kansas City, outscoring the two by a combined 68–10 margin as they traveled to San Diego to play the Chargers with a 9–2 mark despite the injuries and issues they had. The defense once again played well, limiting the home team to only 218 yards of total offense, but Terry Bradshaw had one of the worst games of his career, throwing for only 153 yards with five interceptions as the team also lost three fumbles in a humiliating 35–7 defeat.

Bradshaw rebounded the following week with a career high 364 yards passing as the Steelers racked up an NFL 1979 high 606 yards of total offense against the Browns at Three Rivers. They needed 17 fourth-quarter points, though, including a Bahr 21-yard field goal with 24 seconds left to tie the game at 30 before the Penn State kicker once again won it in overtime, this time from 37 yards out, 33–30. They defeated the Bengals easily for revenge before Houston finally showed they could beat Pittsburgh 20–17, sending the visitors to 11–4 on the season. They ended the year in an impressive fashion with a 28–0 shutout of Buffalo, limiting the Bills offense to 156 yards. The win gave them the Central Division crown by one game over the Oilers, and after a 34–14 shellacking of Miami in the first round of the playoffs—a game they broke out to a 20–0 first-quarter lead and never looked back—they once again played the Houston Oilers in the AFC Championship game at home. This time, it would be a little closer than the 34–5 contest in the ice the year before.

With Pittsburgh up 17–10 late in the third quarter, the case for instant replay, which was not in effect in 1979, was made. The Oilers' Mike Renfro caught a Dan Pastorini pass deep in the end zone for an apparently game-tying touchdown, but referee Donald Orr ruled the catch out of bounds. Replay showed it was in bounds, but since instant replay was not available at the time, Houston was not given the touchdown and went on to lose 27–13.

After the disputed win, Pittsburgh once again found themselves in the Super Bowl. Despite the fact that the game was being played in Southern California against the Los Angeles Rams, it was a surprise that the underdog Rams had made it this far, and the Steelers were a 10$\frac{1}{2}$-point favorite. Los Angeles quarterback Vince Ferragamo gave the Pittsburgh defense fits all afternoon, and as the game turned to the fourth quarter, they found themselves with a 19–17 lead. As it turned out, 1980 would not be kind to the

Pittsburgh Steelers, so this became the final quarter of their 1970s dynasty. They made the most of it. Bradshaw, who won his second consecutive Super Bowl MVP award with 309 yards passing, hit Stallworth on a spectacular 73-yard bomb to go up 24–19. With Los Angeles driving late in the game, Jack Lambert stepped in front of a Ferragamo pass for an interception, setting up another Bradshaw-to-Stallworth long connection, this one for 45 yards. Harris ended the final scoring drive of the Steelers Super Bowl era for a 31–19 comeback victory.

The win gave the Steel City something it wanted so dearly: confirmation that it truly was the City of Champions!

CHAPTER 40

1979: HUGH AND DANNY

By David Finoli

As the University of Pittsburgh captured the 1976 National Championship, it was on the shoulders of Tony Dorsett, who shattered just about every NCAA rushing record imaginable on his way to the Heisman Trophy. The next season, another iconic figure came to the program, a defensive end from Natchez, Mississippi, who was only noticed by Pitt coaches when they were looking at film of running back Ray "Rooster" Jones in high school. The defensive end's name was Hugh Green, and he would go on to challenge Dorsett as the greatest player ever to don a Panther uniform. In 1979, he was entering his junior season when yet another player who would go down as one of the greatest ever in the program came to campus, a quarterback who grew up within walking distance of Pitt Stadium and decided to stay home to play college football instead of signing a baseball contract with the Kansas City Royals. His name was Dan Marino, and the two careers would intersect as Pitt began three-year consecutive streak of 11–1 seasons in what was the greatest sustained stretch since the late 1930s.

As they went into the 1979 season, the team was coming off a disappointing year. They had been ranked the entire 1978 campaign, starting out in the top 10 after a 4–0 start. They lost twice in their following three games before a three-game win streak left them 15ᵗʰ in the nation going into a contest against top-ranked Penn State. They played well in a 17–10 loss to finish the year at 8–3 with a Tangerine Bowl bid against North Carolina State. The

Hugh Green didn't come to the University of Pittsburgh as a five-star, sure-for-stardom recruit, but by the time he left, he had been named consensus first team All-American three times and had his number retired by the school and is generally considered one of the greatest collegiate defensive players in the history of the game. *Photo courtesy of University of Pittsburgh Athletics.*

Wolfpack, surprisingly, manhandled the Panthers 30–17 as they tumbled out of the final top 20 poll, leaving them with more questions than answers in an 8–4 season.

In a preseason scrimmage not long before the season began, they were pretty banged up, especially at wide receiver, where they had to move tight end John Brown to flanker, as they had only one healthy receiver. On defense, Pitt looked to be strong, with Ricky Jackson, future NFL Hall of Famer, lining up opposite of Green with future NFL players Greg Meisner, Bill Neill and Jerry Boyarsky in the middle of what would turn out to be one of the most impenetrable defensive lines in the history of college football. The defensive backfield of Jo Jo Heath, Lynn Thomas, Carlton Williamson, Mike Christ and Barry Compton would also be a strength for the team. The offensive line of Russ Grimm, Mark May, Jim Morsillo, Dan Fidler and Bob Gruber started the campaign in front of Rick Trocano, who had been the starting quarterback the previous season and filled in for Matt Cavanaugh in 1977 when the All-American quarterback was injured. He was thought to be nothing more than a gatekeeper until Marino was ready to go. The backfield of Freddy Jacobs and Randy McMillan was considered formidable but not as spectacular as the ones they had earlier in the decade.

Pitt started off the season at home against Kansas, a team who had finished 1–10 in 1977, and had relatively few problems in a 24–0 victory. McMillan showed he was more than formidable with 141 yards rushing, and Marino made his collegiate debut in relief of Trocano, hitting receiver Ralph Still with a perfect 23-yard touchdown pass, one of three Still had on the day, in the victory. They traveled to Chapel Hill the next week to play a much tougher North Carolina team, and after a 17–7 loss where they turned the ball over seven times, all of a sudden, there were more questions about whether this team could be successful. Defensively, they played well, giving up only 219 yards, but head coach Jackie Sherrill was obviously frustrated with the turnovers. "You can't win a football game giving the ball away like we did," he said in a *Pittsburgh Press* article following the contest.

Pitt, 13th ranked in the Associated Press poll before the loss, found themselves dropping completely out, a situation that wasn't exactly enhanced the following week at Temple when kicker Mark Schubert had to save the day with a fourth-quarter field goal with 3:53 left to give Pitt a narrow 10–9 victory. With Boston College and Cincinnati coming to Pitt Stadium before they traveled to Seattle to meet the nationally ranked Washington Huskies, Sherrill knew his offense needed to get better quickly. He split snaps in each contest with Marino and Trocano as his running game eclipsed 200 yards in both contests with Pitt dominating their two opponents 28–7 and 35–0, respectively.

The Panthers were now on a roll and found themselves back in the top 20 at 17 but were facing two nationally ranked teams in the next two weeks. Playing their best football of the year, Pitt convincingly beat Washington despite four Trocano interceptions in a 26–14 win, a game that saw McMillan score twice and collect 95 yards. The next week, against 17th-ranked Navy, the defense limited the Midshipmen to 155 yards of total offense in a 24–7 win. Marino came in after Trocano pulled his hamstring and showed his vast potential, throwing for 227 yards in the victory.

As it turned out, Trocano was truly the gatekeeper, as the young freshman took over at that point. Following a 28–21 win over Syracuse, they went on a three-game road trip to end the season. It began with the Backyard Brawl at Morgantown, where they won 24–7 before crushing Army 40–0 to push their record to 9–1. Marino was at his best in the two games, throwing for a combined 504 yards. Now ranked 11th, they traveled to State College to play the Penn State Nittany Lions. After the home team went up 7–0 on a Matt Suhey 54-yard run, Pitt shot ahead 10–7 before Curt Warner ran back a kickoff 95 yards to put Penn State back on top 14–10. The game was over at

While Hugh Green might not have been considered a future superstar when he came to Pitt, quarterback Danny Marino was. Marino was the top high school quarterback in the nation when he decided to stay at home and become part of the Panthers program. The Marino era began in earnest his freshman year when he took over the starting reigns as QB from Rick Trocano and helped lead the team to an 11–1 mark and a spot in the Fiesta Bowl. *Photo courtesy of University of Pittsburgh Athletics.*

that point, as we soon found out. Marino passed for 272 yards, and McMillan had arguably the best game of his Pitt career with 114 yards rushing, another 93 receiving and all three Panther touchdowns as Pitt scored the final 19 points of the game in a 29–14 victory that vaulted them into the top 10.

After defeating Army, Pitt had accepted a bid to play in the Fiesta Bowl on Christmas Day. As it turned out, their opponent was less than desirable for a top 10 team who was 10–1. They would play the 6–4–1 Arizona Wildcats, who were playing in their first bowl game in 11 years. The disappointed Panthers were not at their best in this contest as the offense struggled, but Hugh Green and the defense played well in the 16–10 victory, a game where the underdogs often looked like the better team. Despite the poor play in the bowl game, Pitt finished in the top 10, ranked ninth, in what would be the first of three consecutive 11–1 seasons. While seven turnovers against North Carolina cost them an undefeated season and a shot at the national championship, Danny Marino began his era of excellence and Hugh Green continued his, as he was a consensus All-American for the second consecutive time. Eventually, they both would be given the ultimate honor of having their numbers retired by the school as their eras intersected for two seasons that helped bring the Panthers back as an elite program again.

CHAPTER 41

1977, 1979: FUN AT THE FLICKS

TWO PITTSBURGH SUPER '70s FILM FARCES

By Tom Rooney

There have been hundreds of movies, television shows and documentaries filmed in the Pittsburgh area going all the way back to 1897, when Wikipedia states that something called *The Prophecy of the Gargoyle* was released. To whom and about what *Gargoyle* entailed as a movie are mysteries of sorts. The Pittsburgh area has been so active with moviemaking, especially in the last 50 years, that it has been nicknamed "Hollywood on the Mon" in cinematic circles.

Pittsburgh can also claim the world's first theater dedicated solely to movies. In 1905, an entertainment entrepreneur named John Harris opened the Nickelodeon on Smithfield Street in downtown. Harris also founded the American Hockey League Pittsburgh Hornets and the North American touring sensation the Ice Capades. Harris would regularly ink Winter Olympic medal winners and put them on ice for long stretches that were lucrative for all involved.

Many sports movies flavor the Pittsburgh flicks roster. Early on, in 1922, a ditty called *In the Name of the Law* was released, starring, of all people, Honus Wagner. The original version of *Angels in the Outfield* came out in 1952, and the scenes featuring Forbes Field and former Pirates playing small parts are priceless. Some serious subjects were also covered in later Pittsburgh sports films like *Warrior* (2011) and *Concussion* (2015). And in 2022, Amazon released the series *A League of Their Own*, based loosely on the movie about women's professional baseball.

Squaring off are author Tom Rooney (*left*) and Dave Hanson (*right*). Hanson, who currently manages the sports center at Robert Morris University,was a member of the 1975 NAHL champion Johnstown Jets, then was cast in the movie *Slap Shot* as one of the legendary Hanson brothers. In real life, he did eventually play in the NHL, appearing in 33 games. He also was in the WHA, where he played in 103 contests for New England, Minnesota and Birmingham. *Photo courtesy of Tom Rooney.*

But in the Super 1970s, the sports movies made in Pittsburgh were made for laughs!

Slap Shot, filmed largely in the Johnstown, Pennsylvania area and released in 1977, and *The Fish That Saved Pittsburgh* in 1979 weren't at all serious, but for many even today, they are seriously funny. No book on sports in the Pittsburgh area in the Super '70s decade would be complete without what experienced coaches all advocate: film study. Here we go with some hockey and hoops that garnered some heavy chuckles.

SLAP SHOT (1977)

Dave Hanson had heard rumors there might be a movie made around the all-too-real comical characters that played minor league hockey in the mostly small towns in North America in the 1970s. His teammate with the Johnstown Jets was Ned Dowd, whose sister, Nancy Dowd, was a screenwriter. Ned was not the typical fight-infused, let's-drop-the gloves minor league hockey type. He was Boston born with a master's degree. Nancy would soon win an Oscar for cowriting *Coming Home*, the Vietnam War drama that was released in 1979. But first it would be a hockey topic, and the stories Ned shared with her about rough-and-tumble minor league hockey would become the inspiration for a movie titled *Slap Shot*.

Hanson even "read some lines" from Nancy's evolving screenplay while the Jets were still playing late in the 1975 season. She finished the script, and then a major Hollywood director got attached to the project, George Roy Hill, a man whose previous work included blockbusters *Butch Cassidy and the Sundance Kid* in 1971 and *The Sting* in 1974. Hill had won the Oscar for Best Director for the latter, and both films starred Robert Redford and Paul Newman. And it was Newman who would play the player-coach of the mythical Charleston Chiefs in *Slap Shot*, the immortal and somewhat immoral Reggie Dunlop.

It wasn't the ultimate Jack Hanson role that Dave Hanson had begun preparing for in the early days of the moviemaking. He was reading for the part of Dave "Killer" Carlson, but when the real-life hockey player who was supposed to play Jack got called up by the Edmonton Oilers of the WHA for their playoffs, Hanson switched from Killer to one of three Hanson Brothers, and a Hollywood actor was brought in to play his original role. That new Killer was Jerry Houser, who would eventually be best known for acting in a lot of *Brady Bunch* spinoff movies.

The First Summit Arena at the Cambria County War Memorial in Johnstown, Pennsylvania. Formerly called the Cambria County War Memorial Arena, it opened in 1950 and played host to Johnstown's many minor league hockey teams, including the Jets, who won the city's last league hockey title to date. It also was the facility where the iconic hockey film *Slap Shot* was filmed. *Photo courtesy of Tom Rooney.*

"The new 'Killer' was really kind of a 'Pillsbury Doughboy' type of Hollywood guy, much different than who I was at the time but he was great and fit right in," Hanson recalled. "And Jack Carlson, whose spot I took as a 'Hanson Brother,' he never regretted not being in the movie because he had a really solid National Hockey League career. There were a lot of non-hockey types playing roles. The referee, who confronts us after the pre-game fights…and when you hear 'I'm listening to the fucking song'—that actor couldn't skate very well. You'll notice he's filmed from the waistline up. He kept falling down trying to skate and it took forever to shoot. They ended up cutting the takes into sections to make it usable."

The movie was filmed over three months, April through June 1976, largely in and around Johnstown. Many of the city's locals were extras in the movie, and there isn't a person around the city that can't tell a story about their own experience with the Hollywood set or at least that of their parents.

Dave Hanson was a real hockey player and had a modest playing career, but he became even more celebrated and likely will never be forgotten because of *Slap Shot*. Case in point: at an offseason trip to Australia for a health foundation to educate people about concussions, Wayne Gretzky, arguably the greatest player in league history, was paired with Hanson at an autograph event. The line for Hanson's signature was long, *Slap Shot* having been a worldwide hit. Gretzky's line was much shorter. "You better get over to that other line," Hanson prompted the Aussie attendees. "That's the greatest hockey player ever. Me, I scored one NHL goal!"

And Hanson was a hit when visiting a motor sports event where Paul Newman was competing with his new avocation, racing cars. Always interested in autos, Newman's interest accelerated after starring in the 1969 film *Winning*. Newman played a race car driver who aspires to win the famed Indianapolis 500. Hanson was the actor's guest in the pit for a number of races. One day, Hanson spied a very well-known racing figure coming to Newman's camp, and before he could even try to greet his racing hero, Mario Andretti rushed to him and embraced him. "You're one of the Hanson brothers," he gushed. "That's my all-time favorite movie."

Slap Shot was eventually spun into sequels, one a G-rated version youngsters could watch. But it was the real unvarnished, unedited, unapologetic original version that Dave Hanson's son, Christian, first watched as a 12-year-old on a four-hour bus ride with his teammates returning from a youth hockey tournament. From an article Christian penned for the *Players' Tribune*:

> *One of the chaperone parents said "Who wants to watch SLAP SHOT?" Some kids cheered. A few minutes into the movie, I see someone familiar. But what's with the glasses. Wait, is that…my dad? "That's my dad up there!"*

Yes, it was his dad, and his dad had some explaining to do when Christian returned home. "We never talked about *Slap Shot* at home and we were going to wait a few years but one of the hockey parents had other ideas," Dave remembered. "My wife and I had to sit down with Christian and explain that *Slap Shot* was just a fun movie that made fun of some exaggerated hockey characters. That's all."

Slap Shot was a modest hit at the box office in 1977 and finished only 21st in movie gross sales that year. But it's the leader in at least one category: its famous, oft-quoted lines of dialogue. They are often replayed to Dave Hanson when he runs into fans. He still wears his hair long for the many appearances each year he makes around the world where *Slap Shot* has cult status more than four decades after its release. What's the favorite among

Inside the First Summit Arena in a small museum dedicated to the movie *Slap Shot*, which was filmed at the facility. Shown above is a movie poster for the film that includes autographs from the Hanson brothers. *Photo courtesy of David Finoli.*

fans? Hanson replied, "Probably, this one." (He goes into character here.) "Get me a grape and an orange. And none of that stinkin' root beer!"

The Fish That Saved Pittsburgh (1979)

Jack Mathison is a native of the Pittsburgh area. He starred in football at Mt. Lebanon High and also at Ohio University, where he earned a degree in 1972 from one of the first college sports management programs in the country. Sports facilities were in the Mathison family DNA. His dad had been construction manager for Three Rivers Stadium.

Mathison's first job out of school was with what was called the Auditorium Authority of Allegheny County. It owned and operated the Pittsburgh Civic

Arena, which was in the early part of its second decade. The arena was hosting on average more than 200 events a year in spaces that included the Exhibit Hall under the stands, which was really the area's first convention center. Downstairs there could be a car, boat or sportsmen's show, while in the main arena bowl upstairs, simultaneously, there might be a Penguins home game or one of 40 or so major concerts each year.

Mathison did a little of everything when he first started, but by the year 1978, he was in charge of maintaining the booking calendar, which was a Rubik's Cube of juggling all the potential uses of the facilities there on the "Lower Hill." One day, he got the strangest call. "We want to rent the arena for a month," said the voice from Los Angeles on the other line. "A *month*," Mathison thought out loud.

"We're going to make a movie and your arena will be the star of it," the film studio man continued. Mathison was amazed and excited. He would be an important behind-the-scenes cog for a major motion picture. He dutifully brought the idea to the attention of the higher-ups, and because the movie would be filmed in the summer, it might just be possible from a scheduling standpoint, because that was the relatively slow time for indoor venues like the arena. "It was unprecedented for one project to take up so much time but doable," Mathison remembered thinking.

That movie was *The Fish That Saved Pittsburgh* (TFTSP). And today, when Jack Mathison catches the film running on cable channels like NBA TV, he is flooded with memories.

Gilbert Moses may have been a surprise choice to be the director for TFTSP. The only other film to his credit was *Willie Dynamite*, from four years previously. The film review aggregator Rotten Tomatoes shows only two reviews for that movie. Both recognized Moses's talent, as evidenced by his work on Broadway and television, but Jennie Kermode of Eyes for Film wrote, "This is one of those films that's difficult to rate because it's a patchwork of impressive work and spectacular failures."

TFTSP would also be Moses's last film as director, as he died at age 52.

TFTSP is about a mythical pro basketball team named the Pittsburgh Pythons that struggled on and off the hardwood. A ball boy for the team seeks out an astrologer, and her solution is to put together a new lineup of players who were born under the same birth sign, Pisces, as their one star player, Moses Guthrie, played by real-life NBA star Julius Erving. The newly renamed Pittsburgh Pisces win every game from then on, culminating in a championship game where the team arrives from the sky through the arena's open-roof setting.

While the film features some well-known Hollywood types at the time, like Jonathan Winters, Stockard Channing and Flip Wilson, it's the real-life NBA stars who play Erving's teammates and opposing players that have endeared the film to hardcore sports fans. They include Connie Hawkins, who played for two Pittsburgh pro teams, the ABL Rens and the ABA Pipers; Kareem Abdul-Jabbar; Norm Nixon (who played collegiately at Duquesne across the way from the Civic Arena); Spencer Haywood; Chris Ford; and Bob Lanier, among many others.

Oh, about that one-month rental Mathison negotiated for use of the arena? The production ran way over the time allotted, and expenses soared. "The director (Moses) insisted on like 8–10 'takes' on every shot in the movie," Mathison said. "He also didn't like the locker rooms at the arena and had some built on his own off site…and then never used them. We kept hearing they were going to pull him off the movie but they never did. Things ran so late in the late summer/early fall we had to squeeze shooting in between events with the cameras stored wherever we could find room backstage. It got dicey in a lot of ways."

Push nearly came to shove on the final scene, when the Pisces arrived in a hot-air balloon through the open roof. It started to rain. "They insisted we open the roof *now* and I knew the weather was supposed to clear later and I didn't want to expose the basketball floor, the seats and the lights to rain," Mathison said. "The assistant director said, 'We'll call the mayor, we'll call the governor.' I said, 'Fine, here's the phone!'"

TFTSP was not a commercial hit. But it's a guilty pleasure call-up for sports buffs to download, and it appears occasionally on NBA-TV. In 1995, another sports film utilizing the unique roof-opening capability of the Civic Arena, *Sudden Death*, was released. In both, "the Igloo," the arena's nickname, lives on beyond the memories of the venue's five decades of existence. "It was one of a kind," Mathison said. "Thanks to movies, even if they were bad ones, it lives on today."

DAWN KEEZER OVERSEES THE Pittsburgh Film Office, the organization that recruits the region for new television and movie projects. She gets more than her fair share of sports movie inquiries, and she's aware how those projects resonate with the region. "You can take a person out of Pittsburgh but really never take Pittsburgh out of the person," she said. "Sports gave people, especially those who had moved away, the ability to hold on to the city they love. With hundreds of projects in the region through the years, sports are a natural part of our history."

BIBLIOGRAPHY

Newspapers

Boston Globe
Chicago Tribune
Hartford Courant
Johnstown Tribune-Democrat
Newsday
New York Times

Pittsburgh Post-Gazette
Pittsburgh Press
Post-Standard
Press and Sun-Bulletin
Tribune-Review

Magazines

Golf Digest

Sports Illustrated

Websites

Baseball Reference. https://www.baseball-reference.com.
Bleacher Report. https://bleacherreport.com.
Canonsburg Friends. https://canonsburgfriends.blogspot.com.
ESPN. https://www.espn.com.
Hockey Reference. https://www.hockey-reference.com.
HockeyDB.com. https://www.hockeydb.com.

Inside Edition. https://www.insideedition.com.
SABR. https://sabr.org.

Books

Association of Gentleman Pittsburgh Journalists. *Three Rivers Stadium: A Confluence of Champions*. Charleston, SC: The History Press, 2020.
Cope, Myron. *Double Yoi!* New York: Sports Publishing, 2002.
Finoli, David. *Pittsburgh's Greatest Teams*. Charleston, SC: The History Press, 2017.
———. *Pittsburgh's Greatest Athletes*. Charleston, SC: The History Press, 2019.
———. *1976 National Champion Pitt Panthers: Miracle on Cardiac Hill*. Charleston, SC: The History Press, 2021.

Media Guides and Yearbooks

1970, 1971–1980 Pittsburgh Steelers Media Guide
1970–1976, 1978–1980 Pittsburgh Pirates Media Guide
1975–1977 Pittsburgh Penguins Media Guide
1975–1980 Pitt Panthers Football Media Guide

ABOUT THE AUTHORS

Having grown up in Greensburg, Pennsylvania, David Finoli is a passionate fan of Western Pennsylvania sports, which has been the subject of most of the books he has produced. A graduate of the Duquesne University School of Journalism, where he is featured on the Wall of Fame in Duquesne's journalism and multimedia department, Finoli has penned thirty-six books highlighting the stories of the great franchises in this area, such as the Pirates, Penguins, Steelers, Duquesne basketball and Pitt football, to name a few. In one of his latest books, *Pittsburgh's Greatest Players*, he not only ranks the top fifty players in Western Pennsylvania history but also includes a list of every Hall of Fame athlete who represented the area. Winner of *Pittsburgh Magazine*'s Best of the 'Burgh local author award for 2018, Finoli lives in Monroeville, Pennsylvania, with his wife, Vivian. He also has three children, Tony, Cara, Matt; a daughter-in-law, Susan; a son-in-law, Andrew; and three grandchildren, River, Emmy and Ellie.

Tom Rooney had three stretches of duty at the Civic Arena. As an usher while matriculating across the way at Duquesne University, he worked at least 100 events a year for four years (1969–73), a great way to see his beloved Penguins and actually get paid for it. For a decade (1981–90), he worked for the DeBartolo-owned Civic Arena Corporation, running and promoting events and marketing teams like the Pens, soccer Spirit and indoor football Gladiators. He spent four more years (1999–2003) working for Mario Lemieux as president of the Pens. Under the dome was his home away from home.

im Rooney retired from the National Football League and the New York Giants in May 1999. He is a nephew of Pittsburgh Steeler founder Art Rooney. Rooney earned a degree in education and English from Duquesne University and then began a teaching and football-coaching career at Canevin High School in Pittsburgh in 1964. He also served as track coach and athletic director at that school. In 1968, Rooney became an assistant football coach at Villanova University. His 1968 freshman team was 7–0 and was the first undefeated team in Villanova's football history. Rooney joined the University of Rhode Island as an assistant football coach in 1970 and then returned to Villanova in 1971 for his final year of college coaching; he was also that school's director of recruiting that year. Rooney was the director of pro personnel for the Pittsburgh Steelers from 1972 to 1979, during the Steelers' ascendancy to Super Bowl victories. At that time, Rooney received three of the five Super Bowl rings he was to earn. Rooney then spent six seasons as the director of player personnel and assistant director of football operations for the Detroit Lions. The Lions participated in two playoff games and won the 1984 Central Division Championship during that time. Tim joined the New York Giants as director of pro personnel in April 1985 and was a member of that organization when the Giants won the first two of their Super Bowls. Tim and his wife, Mary Ann, resided in Ho-Ho-Kus, New Jersey, from 1985 until 2010 and then returned to their Pittsburgh roots at the end of that year. Mary Ann is also a graduate of Duquesne University. Their son, Michael, is a graduate of the University of Alabama and employed by Citibank in New York. He is married (to Katie) and resides in Middletown, New Jersey. Their daughter, Sarah Breslin, is a Boston College graduate and earned her law degree at St. John's University Law School in New York. She was an associate at the New York law firm of Mayer Brown until she and her husband relocated to Pittsburgh. Tim has served on the Foundation Board of New Concepts Inc., a Bergen County organization dedicated to the needs of those suffering from disabilities. He served as a member of one of the boards of Monmouth University. He served on the board of directors of Bergen Catholic High School in Oradell, New Jersey, and he was a member of the Advisory Council of the College of Westchester. He was a trustee on the board of St. Anthony's High School in Jersey City. After retiring in 1999, Tim served as a consultant with the New York Giants until his return to the Pittsburgh area. Tim was inducted into the Western Pennsylvania Sports Hall of Fame in 2017.

Chris Fletcher, based in Forest Hills, Pennsylvania, is a writer, marketer, fundraiser and all-around swell guy. Chris is the former publisher and editor of *Pittsburgh Magazine*, where he won 14 Golden Quill Awards. Under his direction, the magazine earned the prestigious White Award as the country's top city magazine in 1995 from the City and Regional Magazine Association. Fletcher also teamed up with David Finoli to author two other sports books, *Steel City Gridirons* and *The Steel City 500*. A 1984 graduate of Duquesne University's journalism program, Chris still longs for a decade like the '70s, when it was great to be a teenage sports fan living in the Pittsburgh area.

Pittsburgh native Frank Garland is a longtime journalist, author and college professor with a lifelong passion for baseball. He worked for more than thirty years at several Northern California newspapers and since 2005 has been teaching at Gannon University in Erie, Pennsylvania. His biography of Willie Stargell, *Willie Stargell: A Life in Baseball*, was published in 2013 by McFarland & Company. He is wrapping up his second biography for McFarland, of Pirates Hall of Famer Arky Vaughan.

Visit us at
www.historypress.com